The New Glucose Revolution

Life Plan

The New Glucose Revolution

Life Plan

PROFESSOR JENNIE BRAND-MILLER

AND KAYE FOSTER-POWELL

RECIPES BY LISA LINTNER

HODDER

contents

INTRODUCTION:
HOW THE GLUCOSE REVOLUTION BEGAN 6

PART ONE

LIFE PLAN: TODAY'S NUTRITIONAL NEEDS ON ONE PLATE

CHAPTER 1: The Glucose Revolution 17
CHAPTER 2: Fats: Facts and Fallacies 31
CHAPTER 3: The Omega Story 43
CHAPTER 4: The Benefits of Mediterranean-style Diets 57
CHAPTER 5: The Benefits of Asian-style Diets 73
CHAPTER 6: Paleolithic Nutrition: the High Protein Diet 85

PART TWO

PUTTING LIFE PLAN INTO ACTION

CHAPTER 7: The Life Plan Way of Eating 97
CHAPTER 8: Get Moving! 131
CHAPTER 9: The Life Plan Menus 135

PART THREE

50 LIFE PLAN RECIPES

CHAPTER 10: About the Recipes 153
CHAPTER 11: Snacks, Soups and Salads 157
CHAPTER 12: Pasta, Noodles and Grains 175
CHAPTER 13: Mains and Accompaniments 189
CHAPTER 14: Desserts 207

PART FOUR

THE LIFE PLAN TABLES 214

GLOSSARY 232

INDEX 234

How the Glucose Revolution Began

In 1995, we joined forces with Dr Stephen Colagiuri, an endocrinologist, to write *The GI Factor* (now called *The New Glucose Revolution*), the first book for the general public about the glycemic index of foods. Research on the glycemic index, or what became known as the GI, had become well accepted and clearly showed that different carbohydrate foods had dramatically different effects on blood glucose levels. We believed that it was high time someone brought this story out to the general public. We knew from our own work that understanding the GI of foods made an enormous difference to the diet and lifestyle of people with diabetes. For some it meant, in our experience, a new lease of life.

In the early 1980s Jennie was studying the nutritional composition of Aboriginal bush foods such as acacia seeds and cheeky yam. These foods are unique today because they are uncultivated foods, unlike wheat or potato. Food samples were sent from all over Australia to her laboratory at the University of Sydney for analysis where she took the opportunity to check the metabolic responses they created; that is, how they actually affected blood glucose levels in the body.

The results were telling. Aboriginal bush foods produced only half the blood glucose responses of starchy Western staples like bread and potatoes. So, the question had to be asked: had these traditional foods somehow protected Aborigines from developing diabetes in times past? The answer was yes.

We have now tested the GI of hundreds of foods both singly and in combination with mixed meals and carried out long-term studies on its potential to improve diabetes control. We now know that consuming low GI foods is associated with a lower risk of both type 2 diabetes and coronary heart disease.

Our studies with animal models show that the GI of foods influences the rate at which animals gain body fat and develop

abnormalities in insulin secretion. We have also tested the applications of GI for sporting performance and appetite control. It is now obvious, not only to us but to many expert committees and health authorities around the world, that the GI of foods has enormous implications for **everybody**. It is indeed a 'Glucose Revolution' in that it has changed forever the way we think about carbohydrates.

But, there's more to the story. After the publication of *The GI Factor* (now *The New Glucose Revolution*), we received a great deal of feedback from readers and health professionals. Hardly a day goes by without an e-mail or letter from someone wanting to say thank you and to know more. In particular people wanted to know how the GI carbohydrate story fits in with all the other health messages about fat and protein. And that's why we have written *The New Glucose Revolution Life Plan*—to give readers the key dietary messages of today in one package. Not just the glucose story. But the fat story. The omega story. The protein story.

There's not just one way of eating a healthy diet. What we now know about these different nutritional factors gives us a great deal of flexibility, which is extremely important and helpful in choosing food and food combinations that suit the likes and dislikes of you and your family.

In *The New Glucose Revolution*, we recommended a diet with high carbohydrate content (but low GI) as the optimal diet for most

The GI is a measure of the blood glucose raising potential of foods that contain carbohydrate.

High GI foods (GI > 70; e.g. potatoes, rice bubbles, most breads) raise blood glucose levels the most.

Low GI foods (GI < 55; e.g. pasta, legumes, All Bran™, porridge) raise glucose levels least.

Low GI foods are best for most people most of the time because they reduce the risk of disease.

Low GI foods are the most satiating and help reduce overeating.

Low GI foods help people with diabetes to control their blood glucose levels.

Low GI foods help reduce blood insulin levels and therefore reduce the undesirable effects of insulin resistance (e.g. coronary heart disease, obesity, type 2 diabetes).

High GI foods have applications in sport.

Sugar has an intermediate GI and is not the villain we imagined. In moderate quantities, sugar plays a useful role in the diet, helping to reduce the intake of saturated fat.

How can you find out about the GI of the food you want to eat?

In our books and on our website we include tables that give the GI of the foods that we and other researchers around the world have tested. The University of Sydney has also developed a GI symbol and consumers in Australia and North America will soon know all about the glycemic index of foods via this new GI symbol on food packages. The GI symbol will appear on a range of foods that have been tested for their glycemic index by an accredited testing laboratory. The GI value will appear near the nutrition panel, along with a brief explanation. The symbol has been endorsed and developed in collaboration with Diabetes Australia NSW and the Juvenile Diabetes Foundation Australia. If you'd like to see more foods carrying the symbol, write to the food manufacturer and encourage them to contact the Sydney University Glycemic Index Research Service (SUGiRS) on 02-9351 3759.

Visit our website for more details: www.glycemicindex.com

people most of the time. We emphasised high carbohydrate eating because we were persuaded by the science at the time (and we still are) that this is the best way of eating for health in countries with a sedentary lifestyle like Australia, New Zealand, Canada, the US, the UK and many European countries.

Why The New Glucose Revolution Life Plan?

The prevailing wisdom throughout the past decade has been that a low fat, high carbohydrate diet is associated with less risk of weight gain, obesity, coronary heart disease, diabetes and some types of cancer. High carbohydrate foods are usually rich sources of micronutrients and phytochemicals as well as being bulky, satiating and therefore less likely to be eaten in excess. In our world of labour-saving devices and electronic entertainment, energy expenditure is limited and foods that are filling and satiating and contain less energy make perfect sense. High carbohydrate foods fit the bill.

But, high carbohydrate diets are not what they used to be. Many of the low fat foods now on supermarket shelves have the same energy density (i.e. kilojoules or calories per gram) as the original high fat counterpart. This is because they can contain up to twice the carbohydrate content of the original food. If energy density is the same, then they are no longer the 'fill you up' foods they were meant to be—they offer no real advantage over the high fat alternative (unless they also contain less saturated fat).

Furthermore, there are some respected scientists who feel that high carbohydrate diets can have undesirable effects—in some individuals they produce adverse blood lipids (high triglycerides, low HDL levels) and thereby increase the risk of coronary heart disease. These experts are often proponents of the Mediterranean style of eating, which emphasises olive oil, high intakes of 'good fats' and less carbohydrate.

There are indeed many large studies showing lower risk of coronary heart disease in Mediterranean countries despite their high fat intake. There's more to Mediterranean eating, however, than olive oil. It includes many low GI foods—pastas, legumes, dairy foods, fruits and salad dressings—that lower blood glucose and insulin responses. So one of the major reasons that Mediterranean-style eating lowers the risk of coronary disease is because it lowers the glycemic load; that is, it reduces the overall effect of the diet on blood glucose and insulin.

As long as people don't overeat this relatively high fat diet, there's every good reason to recommend it. Some people would argue that it's more to their taste than the bulky, often fibrous foods characteristic of high carbohydrate, low GI diets.

The purpose of this new book is to expand your healthy eating choices beyond the low GI, high carbohydrate way of eating recommended in *The New Glucose Revolution*. But to do this, you need to know a few more details: some fats are good guys, others—such as saturated fat—are not. We give you the low down on the fat story and show you the best ratio of polyunsaturated, monounsaturated and saturated fats in the diet and how to achieve the magic number.

Furthermore, some polyunsaturated fats are better than others. Which ones? Eating more fat means you need to be more careful about portion sizes so that you don't inadvertently overeat. Most importantly, if you increase your energy expenditure (by being active), you can afford to eat a higher fat diet. Physical activity is a vital part of a healthy lifestyle. You can't be a couch potato and get away with it, no matter how good your diet!

We also give you the protein story. Diets high in protein are all the rage in North America at present and some nutritionists believe there's an element of truth in them. Others dismiss them out of hand on both nutritional and environmental grounds. There's persuasive evidence, however, that humans evolved during the ice ages on a diet that was high in protein, because wild game and seafood, unlike plant food, were in great abundance. This high animal food diet provided not only very high intakes of protein but high intakes of the omega-3 fatty acids, iron, zinc, vitamin A, folic acid and vitamin B12. Interestingly, deficiencies of these same nutrients plague us today primarily because our diets are dominated by grains.

It has been said that 'grains are truly humanity's two-edged sword' (Professor Loren Cordain, University of Colorado). Without grains, we would not be the urbanised, highly developed, technologically literate species we are. But grains also brought famine on a mass scale, malnutrition, short stature, auto-immune diseases (such as coeliac disease) and dental caries. We believe it's worth considering the macronutrient and micronutrient content of paleolithic diets as a background to dietary guidelines in today's world.

The goal of *The New Glucose Revolution Life Plan* is to show you how easy it is to expand your healthy eating choices and give you a clear understanding of the many dietary issues being talked about today. In Part One we describe how *The New Glucose Revolution Life Plan* approach keeps you healthy and fights disease; Part Two looks at how you can put the these ideas into action with menu plans for different ages and lifestyles; Part Three contains 50 delicious low GI recipes; and Part Four includes the invaluable A to Z of foods, their GI value, and carbohydrate and fat content. You will discover that a new, healthier way of eating is both easy and delicious.

JENNIE BRAND-MILLER AND KAYE FOSTER-POWELL

The New Glucose Revolution Life Plan

today's nutritional needs on one plate

PART ONE

Chapter 1—The Glucose Revolution

Chapter 2—Fats: Facts and Fallacies

Chapter 3—The Omega Story

Chapter 4—The Benefits of Mediterranean-style Diets

Chapter 5—The Benefits of Asian-style Diets

Chapter 6—Paleolithic Nutrition: the High Protein Diet

The Glucose Revolution

What if we were to tell you that eating more of certain foods—certain *delicious* foods—would help you lose weight, manage your diabetes and help protect against heart disease? Sound too good to be true? It's not! The foods we're talking about are specific types of carbohydrates. What's so special about these carbohydrates, you ask? Read on.

Worldwide research since the early 1980s has shown us that different carbohydrate foods have dramatically different effects on blood glucose levels. Until very recently, food scientists and nutritionists widely believed that complex carbohydrates, such as rice and potatoes, were slowly digested energy foods that caused only a small rise in our blood glucose levels. Scientists viewed sugars, on the other hand, as villains that caused rapid fluctuations in blood glucose levels. Our glycemic index research has turned all these beliefs upside down and changed the way we think about carbohydrates—forever.

When scientists began to study the actual blood glucose responses to different foods in hundreds of people, they found that many starchy foods (such as bread and potatoes) were digested and absorbed very quickly and that many sugar-containing foods were *not* responsible for high blood glucose levels. That was quite a surprise!

The glycemic index (GI) was developed to rank foods based on their immediate effect on our blood glucose levels. Carbohydrate foods that break down quickly during digestion have the highest GI values because the blood glucose response is fast and high. In other words the glucose (or sugar) in the bloodstream increases rapidly. Conversely, carbohydrates that break down slowly, releasing glucose gradually into the bloodstream, have low GI values. The substance that produces the greatest rise in blood glucose levels is pure glucose itself. Most other foods have less effect when fed in equal amounts of carbohydrate.

The glycemic index of pure glucose is set at 100 and every other food is ranked on a scale from 0 to 100 according to its actual effect on blood glucose levels.

Today we know the GI values of hundreds of different food items that have been tested following the standardised method. The complete table of the GI values of hundreds of foods can be found in Part Four of this book, starting on page 214.

How you can benefit from low GI foods

The slow digestion and gradual rise and fall in blood glucose levels after eating low GI foods has benefits for many people. Foremost, it helps control blood glucose levels in people with diabetes. It also reduces the secretion of the hormone insulin into the blood. So low GI foods benefit people with and without diabetes.

Low GI foods:

- cause lower insulin levels, which makes fat easier to burn and less likely to be stored
- help to lower blood fats
- are more satisfying and reduce appetite
- reduce our risk of developing diabetes and heart disease

These facts are not an exaggeration. They are confirmed results of studies published in prestigious journals by scientists around the world.

CARBOHYDRATE AND INSULIN

The pancreas is a vital organ near the stomach, and its main job is to produce the hormone insulin. Carbohydrate stimulates the secretion of insulin more than any other component of food. The slow absorption of the carbohydrate in our food means that the pancreas doesn't have to work so hard and needs to produce less insulin.

If the pancreas is overstimulated over a long period of time, it may become 'exhausted' and type 2 diabetes can develop in genetically susceptible people. Even without diabetes, high insulin levels are undesirable.

Our bodies need insulin for carbohydrate metabolism but it has a profound effect on the development of many diseases. Medical experts now believe that high insulin levels are one of the key factors responsible for heart disease and hypertension. Insulin influences the way we metabolise foods, determining whether we burn fat or carbohydrate to meet our energy needs, and ultimately determining whether we store fat in our bodies.

Starch and the glycemic index

Starch granules are composed of two types of starch molecule—a highly branched form called **amylopectin** and a straight chain form called **amylose**. The ratio of the two types of starch in the granule is genetically determined and varies from one variety of food to another. Different varieties of corn and rice, for example, have different ratios of amylose to amylopectin.

Food processing alters starch granules, making them more readily digested. Manufacturers usually alter the granules by heating them in water (called gelatinisation), but they may also grind them for the desired effect. During cooking, heat and water make the starch granules swell so that the compact crystalline structure is destroyed. When we make gravy with flour and water, the gradual thickening of the mixture corresponds to starch gelatinisation. Starches with higher amylose content swell more slowly and at higher temperatures because of stronger binding forces within the granules. In the case of very high amylose starches, such as we find in legumes and high amylose rices, much of the amylose remains ungelatinised at the end of cooking and processing. So there is restricted access by the digestive enzymes, which delays overall digestion and absorption.

In general, foods with a high ratio of amylose to amylopectin have lower GI values.

Scientists use just six steps to determine the glycemic index of a food. Simple as this may sound, it's actually quite a time-consuming process. Here's how it works.

1. Scientists ask a volunteer to eat an amount of food that contains 50 grams of carbohydrate. For example, to test boiled spaghetti, the volunteer would be given 200 grams of spaghetti, which supplies 50 grams of carbohydrate (we work this out from food composition tables). Fifty grams of carbohydrate is equivalent to 3 tablespoons of pure glucose powder.

2. Over the next two hours (or three hours if the volunteer has diabetes), we take a sample of their blood every 15 minutes during the first hour and thereafter every 30 minutes. The blood glucose level of these blood samples is measured in the laboratory and recorded.

3. The blood glucose level is plotted on a graph and the area under the curve is calculated using a computer program.

4. The volunteer's response to spaghetti (or whatever food is being tested) is compared with his or her blood glucose response to 50 grams of pure glucose (the reference food).

5. The reference food is tested on two or three separate occasions and from that we calculate an average value. We do this to reduce the effect of day-to-day variation in blood glucose responses.

6. The average glycemic index found in 8 to 10 people is the glycemic index of that food.

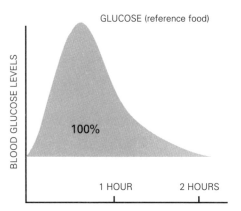

GLUCOSE (reference food)

100%

1 HOUR   2 HOURS

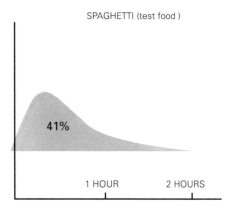

SPAGHETTI (test food)

41%

1 HOUR   2 HOURS

The effect of a food on blood glucose levels is calculated using the area under the curve (hatched area). The area under the curve after consumption of the test food is compared with the same area after the reference food (usually 50 grams of pure glucose or a 50 gram carbohydrate portion of white bread).

KEY FACTORS THAT INFLUENCE THE GLYCEMIC INDEX

COOKING METHODS
Cooking and processing increases the glycemic index of a food because it increases the amount of gelatinised starch in the food. Cornflakes is one example.

PHYSICAL FORM OF THE FOOD
An intact fibrous coat, such as that on grains and legumes, acts as a physical barrier and slows down digestion, lowering a food's glycemic index.

TYPE OF STARCH
There are two types of starch in foods, amylose and amylopectin. The more amylose starch a food contains, the lower the glycemic index.

FIBRE
Viscous, soluble fibres, such as those found in rolled oats and apples, slow down digestion and lower a food's glycemic index.

SUGAR
The presence of sugar, as well as the type of sugar, will influence a food's glycemic index. Fruits with a low glycemic index, such as apples and oranges, are high in fructose.

Sources of carbohydrate

Carbohydrate mainly comes from plant foods, such as cereal grains, fruits, vegetables and legumes (peas and beans). Milk products also contain carbohydrate in the form of milk sugar or lactose, which is the first carbohydrate we eat as infants. Some foods contain a large amount of carbohydrate (cereals, potatoes, legumes are good examples), while other foods, such as carrots, broccoli and salad vegetables, are very dilute sources. The dilute sources can be eaten freely, but they won't provide

anywhere near enough carbohydrate for our high carbohydrate diet. And as nutritious as they can be, salads aren't meals and should be complemented by a carbohydrate-dense food such as bread.

The following foods are high in carbo-hydrate and provide very little fat. Eat lots of them, sparing the butter, margarine and oil during their preparation.

The best low fat, high carbohydrate choices

Cereal grains
These include rice, wheat, oats, barley, rye and anything made from them (bread, pasta, breakfast cereal and flour).

Fruits
A few tasty examples are apples, oranges, bananas, grapes, peaches and melons.

Vegetables
Foods such as potatoes, corn, taro and sweet potato help to create filling, satisfying meals.

Legumes, peas and beans
Baked beans, lentils, kidney beans and chickpeas are a few good choices.

Milk
Not only is milk an excellent source of carbohydrate, it's also rich in bone-building calcium. (Adults should use low fat or skim milk and yoghurt to minimise fat intake.)

We believe that the most appropriate and practical way to put the GI theory into practice is simply to substitute low GI foods for high GI foods. This has the effect of lowering the overall glycemic index of your diet.

The richest sources of carbohydrate are cereal-based foods such as bread, biscuits, bakery products, breakfast cereals, rice and pasta. Potatoes and potato products are also a major source of carbohydrate in Western diets. Choosing low GI varieties of these foods will significantly lower the GI of your diet.

HIGH GI CHOICE	LOW GI ALTERNATIVE
BREAD	
Regular, smooth-textured wholemeal or white	Dense breads containing a lot of whole grains; sourdough and stone ground flour breads
RICE	
Most Australian-grown long and short grain varieties especially sticky rices	Long grain Basmati; Doongara; imported Japonica (Japanese) rice
POTATOES	
Most, including Pontiac, Desiree and Sebago	Sweet potato; yam; taro; new potatoes (these have a moderate GI); pasta of all types; noodles; legumes of all types; whole grains such as barley and bulgur
CEREALS	
Most processed breakfast cereals	Rolled oats, semolina, muesli, certain processed cereals (e.g. All-Bran™ and Guardian™)
BISCUITS	
Most biscuits and crackers	Biscuits made with dried fruit, oats and wholegrains
TROPICAL FRUITS	
Mango, pineapple	Temperate climate fruit such as apples, stone fruit, citrus

How much carbohydrate?

FOOD	PERCENTAGE OF CARBOHYDRATE PER 100 GRAMS
apple	12
baked beans	11
banana	21
barley	61
bread	47
cookie	62
corn	16
cornflakes	85
flour	73
grapes	15
ice-cream	22
milk	5
oats	61
orange	8
pasta	70
peas	8
pear	12
plum	6
potato	12–17
raisins	75
rice	79
split peas	45
sugar	100
sweet potato	17
water cracker	71

The sugar–fat seesaw

Did you know that fat and sugar tend to show a reciprocal or seesaw relationship in the diet? Research shows that diets high in fat are low in sugar, and diets low in fat are high in sugar. But studies over the past decade have found that diets high in sugar are no less nutritious than low sugar diets. This is because restricting sugar is frequently followed by higher fat consumption, and many fatty foods are poor sources of nutrients.

In some cases, high sugar diets have been found to have higher micronutrient contents. This is because sugar is often used to sweeten some very nutritious foods, such as yoghurts, breakfast cereals and milk.

A low sugar (and high fat) diet has more proven disadvantages than a high sugar (and low fat) diet.

LOW GI EATING

Low GI eating means making a move back to the high carbohydrate foods that are staples in many parts of the world. The emphasis is on whole foods such as whole grains and legumes—barley, oats, dried peas and beans—in combination with certain types of breads, pasta, rice, vegetables and fruits. Stock your pantry with these foods and keep a loaf of low GI grain bread in the freezer.

New developments

Since we wrote the second edition of *The GI Factor* in 1998, there have been new developments and further studies suggesting enormous benefits of a low GI-style of eating. In fact, it seems the world has finally caught on to what many Australians knew back in the mid-1990s. The most rewarding part was the release of the American edition of *The GI Factor* in 1999—we called it *The Glucose Revolution* because Americans associate 'GI' with 'GI Joe'! The book gained endorsements from major researchers in the field, including Dr Joanne Manson at Harvard, and spent many weeks on the *New York Times* bestseller list. It's quite an achievement for a scientifically accurate nutrition book.

In early 1998 when The World Health Organisation/Food and Agriculture Organisation released their 'Expert Report on Carbohydrates in Health', 20% of the report was devoted to the glycemic index of foods. In its list of final recommendations is the clear advice that the bulk of carbohydrate-containing foods should be 'those rich in non-starch polysaccharides (dietary fibre) and with a low glycemic index' (www.fao.org/es/esn/carboweb/carbo/pdf).

Now we have released the third major edition of our core book, re-titled *The New Glucose Revolution*. With over 800,000 copies of the series sold in over 12 countries, the 'revolution' is here!

GI and heart disease

The most important new finding came from Harvard University's Nurses Health Study. The study found that the women who ate diets with the highest glycemic index had twice the risk of having a heart attack compared to women with the lowest glycemic index, during a follow-up period of 10 years. These findings follow those of two earlier Harvard-based studies showing that the risk of developing type 2 diabetes is also related to the glycemic index of the diet. Together, these three very large studies involving tens of thousands of people have put the GI in the world spotlight. The question now is, how and why does the GI influence the disease process?

In 1999, a paper published in one of the most prestigious medical journals in the world, *The Lancet*, reported that the glycemic index of foods is an independent determinant of the level of good cholesterol (HDL) in the blood. The higher your HDL levels, the lower your risk of developing cardiovascular disease. The study, based on the dietary analysis of over 1400 randomly selected adults in Britain, found that the lower the GI of the diet, the higher the level of good cholesterol in the blood. Only smoking, body weight status and the GI of the diet were identified as potentially modifiable factors that influenced HDL levels.

This was a startling finding, because the authors were expecting to find that dietary fat was more influential. For over 30 years, the amount and type of fat has dominated research into heart disease and its risk factors. Because of its controversial nature, The Lancet paper was accompanied by an editorial addressing the issue of 'good and bad carbohydrates'. The editorial concluded that further research was needed to prove that the GI of foods affected the HDL concentration.

Fortuitously, the evidence came soon after in the form of an Australian study comparing high and low GI diets as well as a high monounsaturated fat, Mediterranean-style diet. People with type 2 diabetes consumed the three diets in random order for four weeks each. The clearest finding was that HDL—the good cholesterol—was higher on the low GI diet and high monounsaturated fat diet than on the high GI diet.

A study from Sweden, also carried out on type 2 diabetic subjects, made another exciting finding about low GI diets. The investigators compared high and low GI diets that were absolutely identical in every respect except GI. They achieved this by selecting a typical low GI diet based on whole grain products and legumes. To produce the equivalent high GI diet, they simply reduced the particle size of the foods in the low GI diet by milling and mashing! The result was two diets that provided

UNLIMITED VEGETABLES

You can eat most vegetables without thinking about their glycemic index. Most are so low in carbohydrate that they have no measurable effect on our blood glucose levels, but they still provide valuable amounts of fibre, vitamins and minerals. Higher carbohydrate vegetables include potato, sweet potato and corn. Among these, corn and sweet potato are the lower GI choices. Pumpkin, carrots, peas and beets contain some carbohydrate but a normal serving size contains so little that it does not raise our blood glucose levels significantly.

Salad vegetables such as tomatoes, lettuce, cucumber, peppers and onions have so little carbohydrate that it's impossible to test their glycemic index values. In generous serving sizes, they will have no effect on blood glucose levels. Think of them as 'free' foods that are full of healthful micronutrients. Eat and enjoy!

WHY ARE THERE NO GI VALUES FOR MEAT, NUTS AND AVOCADOS?

We are often asked this question. These foods contain no or very little carbohydrate so we can't even test their GI. Essentially, you can regard their GI as zero!

exactly the same nutrient composition (down to the last molecule), but different rates of digestion and absorption. The authors found something that no other group had yet reported. Clotting factors in the blood, which are often abnormal in people with diabetes, were completely 'normalised' on the low GI diet but remained abnormal on the high GI diet. Since the tendency of blood to clot is well known to increase our risk of heart attack, this was a truly important breakthrough.

The GI and obesity

In the world of obesity and overweight, there have been new findings from the Children's Hospital in Boston showing that high glycemic index foods encourage overeating. The subjects were 12 obese teenage boys who were studied on three occasions. On each occasion, in random order, they consumed a breakfast and lunch based on low, medium or high GI foods. All meals had the same energy content, and the high and medium GI meals had the same nutrient composition, fibre content and palatability. For the five hours following lunch they were allowed to eat when and what they wanted. Changes in hormones and metabolic markers were measured throughout the day.

The investigators found that voluntary energy intake was 80 per cent greater after the higher GI meals and 50 per cent

greater after the medium GI meals than that seen after the low GI meals. The authors concluded that the rapid absorption of carbohydrate after eating high GI foods induces a sequence of hormonal and metabolic changes that promote excessive food intake in obese subjects.

The GI and sport

It is clear that GI has taken off in the vocabulary of both the sports physiologists and sports enthusiasts, especially those in the United States. High GI foods are being recommended specifically during and after events to maintain and replenish muscle glycogen stores. Two studies have confirmed our earlier finding that low GI foods prolong endurance in cyclists. The low GI food in these studies has been porridge oats and, not surprisingly, the research has been funded by the Quaker Oats company. Admittedly, there have been negative reports in which low GI foods have not offered any advantage over high GI foods, but in these cases a 'time trial' (for instance, distance travelled or work expended in a set time) was the basis for comparing foods. Perhaps this indicates that low GI foods offer benefits in activities that rely on endurance rather than speed. We must await further research under field conditions to confirm the advantage of low GI foods.

Cereals and grains are the major source of energy and protein for humanity today, but they were not a part of the diet that we evolved on millions of years ago. Findings from the archaeological record 15 000 years ago herald the beginnings of humankind's use of cereal grains for food. As populations increased, resources of mammals, fish and birds became depleted and the demand on agriculture increased. The last 10 000 years has seen an increased reliance on cereals for food—with consequent developments in processing from crude grinding between stones, which yielded small amounts of coarse meal, to high-speed roller milling yielding tonnes of fine white flour. There are many nutritional implications of this change in the human diet, one of which has been an increase in the GI Modern methods of cereal processing transform the low GI carbohydrate of cereal grains to high GI foods. To eat a low GI diet we encourage you to use less heavily processed cereal products and more wholegrain cereals.

BREADS

One of the most important changes you can make to lower the GI of your diet is to choose a low GI bread. These include:

WHOLEGRAIN BREADS

Wholegrain breads contain lots of 'grainy bits'. Where the fibrous seed coat of cereal grains is intact it acts as a physical barrier to slow starch digestion. In some wholegrain breads, such as Bürgen™ breads, the low GI may also result from the use of a long fermentation time in the preparation of the dough. During this process the yeast consumes the quickly digested starch, converting it to energy, carbon dioxide (to make the bread rise) and a little alcohol, which evaporates during baking. What the yeast leaves behind is the more slowly digested starch.

PUMPERNICKEL
This is a true wholegrain bread, being made from whole rye grains.

STONE GROUND FLOUR AND SPROUTED WHEAT BREADS.
These have been tested in Canada and found to have low GI values, probably due to their content of coarsely milled and intact grains.

SOURDOUGH BREADS
The reduced blood glucose and insulin levels observed after ingestion of sourdough breads highlighted to researchers the potential of acids in foods to reduce the GI. In sourdough breads lactic acid and propionic acid, produced by the natural fermentation of starch and sugars by yeast, is believed to lower the GI by slowing stomach emptying.

CHAPATI (BAISEN BASED)
Chapati is an unleavened bread widely eaten in India and the Indian subcontinent. While it is often made with wheat flour, it is also made from baisen, or chickpea flour, which is milled from a small variety of chickpeas. Chapati made from baisen has a significantly lower GI than that made from wheat flour due to the nature of the starch.

A final word

The potential importance of GI in sports performance and in the management of both obesity and heart disease is where the research is now heading. It is remarkable that many of the studies are now emanating from the United States, one of the last bastions of opposition to the GI. It is probably true to say that the GI approach, which started out as an idea with possible relevance to the management of diabetes, has become the most enduring, inspiring, universally applicable dietary concept to arise in the last 20 years of the 20th century. The glycemic index has come of age!

THE TAKE-HOME MESSAGE

- The glycemic index of foods is for **everybody**, including those with diabetes
- Low GI foods result in slow and sustained release of glucose into the blood
- High GI foods result in quick release of glucose into the blood
- Low GI foods are best for most people most of the time

Chapter 2

Fats:
Facts and Fallacies

Much has been written about fats and oils in our diet, some of it rather too scientific and confusing. But it's true that the type of fat we eat determines, to a large degree, whether we will suffer a heart attack or stroke. What's more, we are now learning that the *right* type of fat in our diet (even if it's a low fat diet) may reduce our risk of certain types of cancer, depression, many auto-immune diseases such as arthritis, and may generally promote health and longevity. Indeed, there is good evidence that the type of fat an infant receives in its first few weeks of life may increase intelligence and learning ability.

One of the main findings of the past decade is that not all fats are bad; in fact, some fat must and should be eaten for optimal health. In our quest for a non-fattening diet, we have unwittingly thrown out the baby with the bath water. Many of us decided that all fats were bad and that a healthy diet contained as little fat as possible. This is absolutely incorrect. It is possible to replace the harmful fats with the beneficial ones, which allows us to consume as much as 35 to 40 per cent of our energy as fat. For many people, this higher fat diet is much more palatable than the high carbohydrate regime currently recommended by most health experts. The latter way of eating fails for many people—not because it doesn't work, but because they don't like it and therefore don't follow it for any length of time. A diet higher in fats, that is in good fats, is likely to be more acceptable in some groups because it more closely matches past eating habits, ingrained since childhood.

The good and the bad about fats

Most people have heard that saturated fat isn't good for us. There's no argument from anybody on this one. Saturated fat comes in the form of selvedge fat on meat, the cream in milk and other high fat dairy products, and in some of the tropical oils such as palm oil, widely used as shortening for frying and for making cakes, pies and biscuits. Many studies from all around the world have shown that saturated fat clearly increases our risk of coronary heart disease (heart attack). But don't make the mistake of thinking animal foods are all bad just because some contain saturated fat. In

WHICH OIL FOR WHAT?

We recommend using a variety of different oils, depending on the dish:

- For stir-fries, add a distinctive flavour with sesame oil or canola-based flavoured oils.

- For salad dressings you can add a nutty flavour with walnut, macadamia or mustard seed oil, or use some sesame oil for an oriental salad.

- For Mediterranean cooking, including salads, we suggest extra virgin and virgin olive oil for its distinctive flavour.

- For everyday cooking, including roasting and frying, choose a neutral flavoured oil with a high smoke point, such as sunola or canola. For a pleasant nutty flavour in baked goods try mustard seed oil.

fact, as we explain in Chapter 6, humans evolved on a steady diet of animal foods and we are dependent on them to get many of the nutrients we need. In our evolutionary past, however, animal foods were not as high a source of saturated fat as they are nowadays. Game meat, even today, is lower in fat and has relatively less saturated fat compared with that of domesticated animals.

When animals are confined so that they can't move around naturally and are over-fed a diet of grains, they gain an excess of body fat that is deposited in and around the muscles. Grain-fed meat is typically what we find in America today: it is highly marbled (that is, it has fat within the muscle tissue that is impossible to avoid eating) and, to most Americans, this equates with high quality, good eating meat. It might taste good, but it is extremely high in saturated fat. In Australia, where the majority of meat production comes from pasture-fed animals, the fat content within the muscles is almost as low as in game meat (about 5 per cent). As long as the selvedge fat is not eaten, the rest of the meat is lean and highly nutritious.

Recently, trans-fatty acids have been identified as being just as bad as saturated fats. Trans-fatty acids are produced during the manufacture of margarines and behave like saturated fat both in the product (increasing its firmness) and in the human body (increasing the risk of heart attack).

Many people these days are doing a good job in reducing their fat intake by using less fat in food preparation, choosing low fat dairy foods and buying leaner cuts of meat. But is this the best we can do? While these are healthy habits, much of the fat we eat is coming from foods that aren't prepared by us.

Consider these examples:

Potato crisps 15 grams of fat per 50-gram packet (average)

Milkshake with ice-cream 17 grams of fat

Instant noodles 20 grams of fat per packet (average)

Chocolate bar 20 grams of fat

Ice-cream on a stick (e.g. Magnum, Heaven) at least
20 grams of fat each (average)

Extra large muffin 20 grams of fat

2 plain doughnuts 20 grams of fat

Popcorn at the movies 24 grams of fat in a large bucket

Oven-baked muesli slice 25 grams of fat in a 90-gram piece

Sweet and sour pork with fried rice at least 35 grams of fat per serve

Medium burger and fries 40 grams of fat or more

Fettucine carbonara 45 grams of fat per serve

2 pieces of fried chicken and chips 48 grams of fat

Americans have had a lot of bad press about trans-fatty acids—and rightly so, because their diet contains large amounts. In fact, many Americans have gone back to eating butter because they figure they may as well enjoy their saturated fat. Australians have been somewhat lucky in this regard because our margarine manufacturers have always tried to limit the formation of trans-fatty acids and now there is less than ever.

What surprises many people is that some fats are good for us and that a healthy diet includes these fats. Monounsaturated fats, such as those in olive and canola oil, can reduce the risk of cardiovascular disease by reducing triglycerides in the blood and increasing the good HDL cholesterol. This is especially important if you have diabetes or a family history of heart disease. It turns out that a low HDL level is one of the very best predictors of increased risk of heart attack. In a French study known as the Lyon Heart Study, subjects who had already survived at least one heart attack were assigned to two dietary groups. One was given advice on eating the American Heart Foundation diet (that is, low fat, high carbohydrate). The other group was instructed on how to follow a higher fat but Mediterranean-style diet with large amounts of olive oil, fish, fruits and vegetables. The Heart Foundation diet was 30 per cent fat, while the Mediterranean diet was 35 per cent

fat. The results of the study were quite stunning: there were 75 per cent fewer deaths in the group on the Mediterranean-style diet. In fact, after two years the investigators were obliged to discontinue the study because it would have been unethical to continue. Later chapters in this book give you the knowledge, tools and recipes to follow the same type of diet as in the Lyon Heart Study.

Many people are even more surprised to learn that we have a compulsory requirement for some types of fats—those we can't synthesise in our own bodies—called essential fatty acids. They can be obtained only from our diet. We used to think a very small amount of these fatty acids would do but we were wrong. Humans appear to need much larger amounts to function properly and reach their genetic potential. The essential fatty acids play a fundamental role in cell membranes and are needed for normal growth, development and maintenance. The human brain has a high requirement for two of the most important essential fatty acids, called EPA (eicosapentenoic acid) and DHA (docosahexanoic acid). Without them, we can suffer in the body tissues that have a high turnover rate, such as the skin, the earliest sign being a scaly dermatitis. We die if the deficiency exists for longer than a few months. But that's not all. We also appear to need them to achieve the best of mental health and to

'We buy everything light.'
Hardly a week goes by in dietetic practice where we don't hear these words from a patient. So convincingly are foods marketed these days that many of us automatically reach out for that package or bottle that carries the word 'light'. There is light milk, margarine, juice, jam, ham, cheese, chocolate, crackers... The list goes on and on. But it pays to be informed about what food label claims actually mean.

'LOW FAT' means the food must not contain more than 3 grams of fat per 100 grams of food, or 1.5 grams of fat per 100 millilitres of liquid. For example, low fat milk must contain less than 1.5 grams of fat per 100 millilitres. Regular milk contains 4 grams of fat per 100 millilitres.

'REDUCED FAT' means the food must not contain more than 75 per cent of the total fat of a comparable food. For example, reduced fat cheese often contains 25 per cent less fat than regular cheese; however, this doesn't necessarily make it a low fat food.

'FAT FREE' can appear on a food containing less than 0.15 grams of fat per 100 grams of food.

'CHOLESTEROL FREE' does not have the same meaning. To be labelled 'cholesterol free' a food must not contain more than 3 milligrams of cholesterol per 100 grams of food and must be either a low fat food or be low in saturated fat. For example, canola oil is cholesterol free and contains only 8 per cent saturated fat, but it is not fat free.

'LIGHT' or **'LITE'** may refer only to the colour or flavour of a food (although by law this should be clear from the label). It may also be used with terms like 'low fat' or 'reduced fat' and should, in these cases, fit the guidelines for these terms. Take care with the label claim 'light' because many 'light' foods that are reduced in fat have a similar kilojoule content to their regular counterpart, thanks to additional carbohydrate. Also, for every 'light' food that arrives on the market there is another full fat food to seduce us. Think about all the fat free salad dressings that are available right next to the fried salad croutons. And how often have you justified eating an extra serving, because, after all, it is 'light'?

reach our full genetic intelligence potential. Depression has also been linked to a lack of these special fatty acids in our diet.

The best source of EPA and DHA is seafood, especially those fish we call fatty fish (in truth they are actually no fattier than lean meat). Our absolute dependency on these fatty acids may hark back to our evolution on the land–water interface where fish and shellfish were eaten in great abundance. The huge middens (refuse heaps) around the Australian coastline are evidence of this large intake of shellfish by hunter–gatherer Aborigines.

Many experts believe infants do not receive sufficient EPA and DHA in infant formulas and therefore recommend supplements. Breast milk is a good source of these special fatty acids, and Japanese women, whose normal diet includes fish on a regular basis, produce milk with the highest level of all.

The message here is that you might be among the majority of the population who are not eating enough essential fatty acids in their current diet.

In our first book, *The GI Factor* (now *The New Glucose Revolution*), we emphasised the widely accepted recommendation to increase carbohydrate intake (to around 55 per cent of the energy we derive from our diet) and to choose low GI versions of the high carbohydrate foods. The remaining energy in our diet (45 per cent of it) is therefore split between protein and fat. Chances are you are probably eating about 15 per cent of your energy as protein— most people eat this amount without even trying. This still leaves plenty of room for some fat: 30 per cent of energy as fat is still considered a low fat diet. We do not believe it is necessary to eat less fat than this—the diet becomes very bulky and you can miss out on some of the things that have important effects on your health. It's important not to throw out the good fats with the bad fats—and that's exactly what many people have been doing in their quest for the ultimate low fat diet. The good fats include the monounsaturated fats and the omega-3 fatty acids that are found only in certain foods.

Some facts about fats

Fatty acids consist of chains of carbon and hydrogen atoms bonded together. These can vary enormously in length. Milk fat (butter, cheese, cream) and coconut fat tend to contain short ones, fish tends to contain the longest ones. The longer the length of the fatty acids, the more liquid in nature the fat becomes. Thus cheese and coconut fat are solid at room temperature but fish oil, such as cod liver oil, is liquid.

Fatty acids are described as being saturated, monounsaturated or polyunsaturated. This is determined by the

It is a myth that all vegetable oils are good for health. While it's true that all vegetable oils are cholesterol free, their fatty acids can be highly saturated and they can therefore promote high blood cholesterol. Coconut and palm oils, for example, are highly saturated vegetable fats. Most other plant oils contain little saturated fat; for example, avocados, and peanut and other nut oils are largely monounsaturated.

nature of the bonds along the carbon chain. These bonds may be single or double bonds. The presence of only single bonds means that the fat is saturated (that is, saturated with hydrogen atoms) while one double bond in the whole fatty acid means that it is a monounsaturated fatty acid. If there is more than one double bond, the fatty acid is polyunsaturated. The amazing thing is that the presence or absence of one or more double bonds has not only important effects on the characteristics of the fat, it has significant effects on your health.

Saturated fats (that is, triglycerides containing mostly saturated fatty acids), such as we find in dairy products and in selvedge fat on meat, are hard at room temperature, while unsaturated fats are liquid at room temperature. The double bonds allow flexible movement of the hydrogen atoms around the carbon skeleton and therefore the more liquid nature.

Animal fats from ruminant animals (sheep and cattle) are largely saturated. Fats from other animals (e.g. pigs and chickens) are less saturated and contain some polyunsaturated fatty acids. Fats from game animals (e.g. kangaroo, deer) are lower still in saturated fats and often contain significant amounts of polyunsaturated fatty acids. Fats from fish are highly polyunsaturated.

The last bit of chemistry you need to know is the difference between omega-3 and omega-6 fatty acids. Both of these are polyunsaturated fatty acids and are essential in the human diet. Polyunsaturated

THE P:M:S RATIO

When we talk about the P:M:S ratio, we are talking about the proportions of polyunsaturated, monounsaturated and saturated fats in a particular food. The aim is to have more polyunsaturated and monounsaturated fats than saturated fats, so a healthy P:M:S ratio should contain higher numbers for the P and M than for the S.

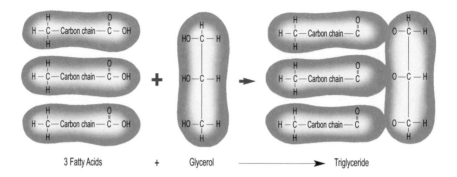

| 3 Fatty Acids | + | Glycerol | ⟶ | Triglyceride |

Most of the fat in food is in the form of triglycerides containing a backbone glycerol molecule and three fatty acids attached. Different types of fats contain different types of fatty acids. It's important to include monounsaturated and polyunsaturated fats, especially long chain omega-3, in out diet because of the important health benefits they offer.

margarines and seed oils, such as safflower, sunflower and soybean oils, are the major sources of omega-6 fatty acids in the Australian diet. Fish and other seafoods are the main source of omega-3 fatty acids; canola oil is the next main source. These two fatty acids differ only slightly in their structure. Omega-3 fatty acids have the first double bond occurring after the third carbon atom from the tail end of the fatty acid. Omega-6 fatty acids have the first double bond occurring at the sixth carbon atom from the tail end. Believe it or not, this makes a big difference to how the fatty acid is used by the body. We need both types of fatty acids in our diet, but many experts believe that our current diets in Western countries are too heavily weighted in favour of the omega-6 series. In Chapter 3, we tell you more about the omega story.

The best types of fat to consume are those containing a high proportion of monounsaturated, polyunsaturated and very long chain omega-3 polyunsaturated fatty acids. In practice, this means meals prepared with lean meat, seafood, olive oil, canola oil, mustard seed oil and Sunola™ oil (these contain a lot of monounsaturated fatty acids). Nuts, avocados and polyunsaturated oils such as safflower oil and sunflower oil can also be included. These foods and oils should take the place of saturated fats, such as we find in fatty meat, fried foods, high fat dairy products and most bakery products. Many of the recipes in the third part of this book can help you achieve the ideal fatty acid proportions in your diet.

The table on pages 40 and 41 shows the amounts of saturated fatty acids, and omega-6 and omega-3 fatty acids in various fats and oils. You will find a table showing the polyunsaturated fat content of many Australian foods at the end of Chapter 3.

Dairy foods are frequently seen in both good and bad lights. They are a rich, readily absorbed source of calcium but can be high in saturated fat. To meet calcium requirements, 2–3 serves of dairy product are recommended daily for adults. Low fat milks and yoghurts are suitable and acceptable to most palates but low fat cheese is generally less palatable and less popular. Here are some tips to make the most of cheese:

Consider a little of a strong flavoured cheese rather than a lot of something bland and tasteless.

Some freshly shaved parmesan is delicious with pasta and is super high in calcium.

Enjoy full fat cheeses in small amounts. This includes regular types of cheddar, blue vein, brie, colby, cream cheese, gouda, havarti. Try grating hard cheeses to make them go further and serve your favourite soft cheeses with low fat crackers, and fresh and dried fruit.

Try some mozzarella cheese for melting—
it contains less fat than many reduced fat cheeses and tastes better.

Lower fat cheeses like cottage cheese (including creamed cottage), ricotta and quark are suitable to use daily.

THE TAKE-HOME MESSAGE

■ A low fat diet is not a no-fat diet.

■ It is more important to avoid saturated fat than to avoid all fats.

■ Choose lean meat and low fat dairy products and be aware of concealed fats in foods.

Figures shown are in grams per 100 grams. The letters 'tr' mean only a trace of the particular fat is found in that food.

Oil/Fat	Omega-6	Omega-3	Long chain omega-3 equivalent	Saturated fat	Comment
Butter	1.7	0.6	0.1	54	Tastes great but is high in saturated fat and cholesterol.
Canola oil	20	10	1.5	8	A good balance of omega-6 to omega-3 and low in saturates
Canola margarine	12	5	0.8	11	Low in saturated fat and makes a small contribution to omega-3 intake
Copha	0.3	0	0	92.4	Coconut oil is primarily saturated fat. As coconut is from a plant, it is cholesterol free
Corn oil	52	2	0.3	14	High in omega-6
Flaxseed/ linseed oil	16	57	8.6	8	Highest plant oil source of omega-3 but very unstable and easily goes rancid
Ghee	1.7	0.9	1.4	65.7	Clarified butter, meaning the milk solids and salt have been removed. High in saturated fat and cholesterol

Oil/Fat	Omega-6	Omega-3	Long chain omega-3 equivalent	Saturated fat	Comment
Mustard seed oil	29	15.4	2.3	5.5	A cold-pressed Australian oil that is very low in saturates and a good source of omega-3
Olive oil	10	tr	tr	14	Omega neutral, great flavour, especially in Mediterranean-style cooking
Palm oil	10	tr	tr	51	A tropical oil widely used in the food industry. High in saturated fats
Peanut oil	34	2	0.3	19	Favoured in Asian cooking, predominantly monounsaturated
Sunola™	8	0	0	10	An omega neutral oil like olive oil. Withstands high temperatures so is good for frying
Soybean oil	54	8	1.2	15	Primarily poly-unsaturated, it contains a reasonable amount of omega-3 and is also high in omega-6 fats

Chapter 3

The Omega Story

Omega-3 fats are polyunsaturated fatty acids found in several plants and plant oils, for example canola, mustard seed, walnuts, linseeds and soy, and in even greater quantities in fish and other seafood. There is strong evidence that omega-3 fats are beneficial in specific aspects of human health.

Several studies have shown that regular fish consumption is consistently associated with reduced risk of coronary heart disease. In fact, one serving of fish per week has been found to reduce our risk of a fatal heart attack by 40 per cent. Higher intakes do not appear to confer greater benefits. The likely protective components of fish are the long chain marine omega-3 polyunsaturated fatty acids called EPA (eicosapentenoic acid) and DHA (docosahexanoic acid). Omega-3 fatty acids derived from plants (plant omega-3 fatty acids, such as canola oil) may also decrease the risk of heart attack, but the effect is not as strong as with the marine fatty acids. Many experts believe there is a

relative deficiency of omega-3 fatty acids in the diet of a large proportion of our population.

Scientists are still trying to work out how omega-3 fatty acids help in preventing heart attack. Several risk factors are reduced in response to consuming more omega-3 fats; for example, at high doses, marine omega-3 fatty acids have been shown to lower triglyceride levels in the blood (high levels of triglycerides are a recognised risk factor for heart disease). They may also slightly raise levels of HDL—the good cholesterol—in the blood. These effects are specific to marine sources of omega-3 fats and are not seen with the plant omega-3 fatty acids.

Some studies suggest marine omega-3 fatty acids reduce blood clotting. Although we want blood to clot quickly when we are wounded, an excessive blood-clotting tendency has been linked to the formation of clots inside the blood vessels—that is, thrombosis. One of the common precipitating events of a heart attack is the formation of a blood clot in an artery of the heart. A clot in a major coronary artery can completely cut the blood supply to a vital part of the heart's muscle, which then loses its ability to pump blood to the brain. The result is death within minutes. Clots in less important arteries can mean the patient survives the attack but the risk of another is high.

Omega-3 fats may also reduce susceptibility to irregular heartbeat, known as heart arrhythmia or ventricular fibrillation. This is one of the main causes of sudden death after an acute heart attack. In studies around the world, omega-3 has been demonstrated to restore regular beating in isolated heart cells.

High intakes of omega-3 fatty acids can also reduce blood pressure in people with raised blood pressure, that is, hypertension. However, this effect can only be found with very high intakes of fish oil supplements, not the amounts that might be consumed through the consumption of fish.

ARTHRITIS

In clinical trials, marine omega-3 fatty acids consistently reduce pain and morning stiffness associated with rheumatoid arthritis. There are certain substances in the blood called eicosanoids and cytokines which initiate the immune response and its consequent inflammation. It is believed these reactions are decreased by omega-3 fatty acids.

ASTHMA AND PSORIASIS

There is no solid evidence that omega-3 fatty acids are effective in treating asthma, and only weak evidence that they are effective in treating psoriasis. Further research is necessary before we can make recommendations here.

BRAIN DEVELOPMENT

Omega-3 fatty acids are important for the growth of nerves in the foetus and young infant. Some experts believe that infants are not able to synthesise enough DHA (docosahexanoic acid) for their needs from the precursor compound ALA (alpha-linolenic acid) for optimal growth. Breast milk, however, is naturally rich in DHA, and DHA levels in the brains of breast-fed babies are higher than those in formula-fed infants. Formulas enriched with DHA have been found to improve visual acuity and neuro–mental development in premature infants compared with conventional formulas. However, the long-term implications of adding DHA to formula are unknown and some infant formula manufacturers are unwilling to risk the safety of the formula by adding it. This is one more reason why human milk should be made available to all infants whether full- or pre-term. Pregnant and lactating women can increase their intake of omega-3 by eating more fish. Pregnant women will pass the benefit on to their infant by way of the placenta, and lactating women by way of their milk.

OMEGA-3 FATTY ACIDS AND CANCER

Many epidemiological studies show an association between high consumption of fish and reduced risk of cancer of the colon and the breast. In addition, experiments in animal models have shown that high doses of marine oils inhibit the development of chemically induced mammary and colo-rectal cancers. However, the experts say that the current evidence is insufficient to prove that eating fish decreases cancer risk.

Does the ratio of omega-3 to omega-6 fatty acids matter?

Experts disagree about the importance of the ratio of omega-3 to omega-6 fats in the diet. Some believe it is too low, that we eat too few of the omega-3 fats and too many of the omega-6 fats from oils such as safflower and sunflower and their respective margarines. Most agree that we need to increase our consumption of omega-3 fats—but do we really need to simultaneously reduce consumption of omega-6 fatty acids? It is this that is controversial. Other experts argue against the use of any ratio.

It is certainly true that increasing the ratio by raising the omega-3 fat intake is not the same as increasing it by lowering the omega-6 fat intake. This is because the protective effect of the omega-6 fat on coronary heart disease is well established and it would be undesirable to reduce these fats.

Intake of long chain polyunsaturated fatty acids during human evolution

Paleolithic diets (that is, what we ate during the long period of human evolution before the development of agriculture) provided two to three times the meat consumed by current affluent nations (see Chapter 6). This means that early human beings ate much more of the omega-6 series of fatty acids. However, the omega-3 fatty acids such as DHA and EPA, which counter the effects of omega-6 fatty acids, were also important constituents of the pre-agricultural diet. High levels of omega-3 fatty acids appear to modulate the thrombotic potential of increased omega-6, so that there is a net anti-thrombotic potential. The omega-3 to omega-6 ratio during the paleolithic era is estimated to have varied from 1:1 to 1:4. Altogether, about 3 grams of long chain polyunsaturated fatty acids would have been consumed each day. EPA consumption has been estimated at 400 milligrams per day and DHA at 270 milligrams per day.

Concerns with omega-3 fats

One of the concerns people have about the omega-3 fatty acids is their susceptibility to oxidation. This is the chemical process that occurs when fats turn rancid. Oxidised fats have been implicated in causing atherosclerosis, or hardening of the arteries. In fact, all polyunsaturated fats are susceptible to oxidation and should be consumed with adequate amounts of antioxidants such as vitamin E. In nature, all polyunsaturated fatty acids are rich sources of vitamin E, but sometimes food processing can inadvertently reduce antioxidant concentrations. This is one reason why we should avoid foods and oils that have been stored for long periods of time (even if stored in the freezer) or under inappropriately high temperatures.

So what's the conclusion?

There is more than enough evidence that marine omega-3 fatty acids can be beneficial to health. This is particularly important for people with coronary heart disease. Plant and marine sources of omega-3 have distinct physiological effects, so they cannot replace each other. Our recommendations are to eat fish at least once a week, as well as including a plant source of omega-3, such as canola or mustard seed oil, in your diet. Olive oil is not a rich source of omega-3 fatty acids. To increase the plant omega-3 fatty acids further, aim to eat green leafy vegetables on a daily basis.

THE BEST FISH SOURCES OF LONG CHAIN OMEGA-3 FATS

Both canned and fresh fish are rich sources of omega-3 fats. The following lists show some of the richest varieties:

CANNED FISH
Salmon (including Australian, pink and red)
Sardines
Mackerel

FRESH FISH
Atlantic salmon (fresh and smoked)
Blue and Spanish mackerel
Gemfish
Sea mullet
Tailor
Southern bluefin tuna
Swordfish

SHELLFISH
Sydney rock oysters, arrow squid and southern calamari

THE TAKE-HOME MESSAGE

■ Modern diets contain too little of the omega-3 types of fat.

■ Omega-3 fats have many health benefits, including a reduced risk of coronary heart disease.

■ Choose canola oil for cooking and salad dressings because of its high omega-3 content.

■ Eat fish once a week, especially those varieties containing more omega-3 (e.g. salmon, tuna).

■ Substitute the 'body egg' for ordinary eggs because it has a naturally high content of omega-3 fats.

The health benefits of omega-3 and omega-6 polyunsaturated fatty acids (PUFAs) are widely acknowledged. The table below lists the total omega-6 and omega-3 fatty acid content of foods, and gives an estimate of the amount of long chain omega-3 PUFAs that will be derived from the alpha-linolenic acid content (long chain omega-3 equivalent) of these foods.

Abbreviations
tr = trace   wt = weight   av = average

TYPE OF FOOD	OMEGA-6 FATTY ACIDS (G)	OMEGA-3 FATTY ACIDS (G)	LONG CHAIN OMEGA-3 FATTY ACID EQUIVALENT (G)
FATS, SPREADS AND OILS			
Beef dripping, 1 tablespoon (20 g)	0.4	0.2	0.02
Blended polyunsaturated oil, 1 tbsp (18 g)	8.6	1.2	0.2
Butter, regular, 1 tbsp (18 g)	0.3	0.1	0.02
Butter, reduced-fat, 1 tbsp (18 g)	0.1	0.05	0.01
Canola oil, 1 tbsp (18 g)	3.6	1.8	0.3
Copha, 1 tbsp (20 g)	0.06	0.0	0.0
Corn oil, 1 tbsp (18 g)	9.4	0.4	0.05
Cottonseed oil, 1 tbsp (18 g)	10.4	0.0	0.0
Dairy Blend, regular or reduced-fat (18 g)	2.5	0.09	0.01
Devondale Dairy Canola, 1 tbsp (18 g)	1.0	0.5	0.07
Devondale Dairy Soft, 1 tbsp (18 g)	2.8	0.1	0.02
Flaxseed (Linseed) oil, 1 tbsp (18 g)	2.9	10.3	1.5
Ghee, 1 tbsp (20 g)	0.3	0.2	0.03
Lard, 1 tbsp (18 g)	1.5	0.02	0.003
Maize oil, 1 tbsp (18 g)	9.7	0.1	0.02

POLYUNSATURATED FAT CONTENT OF AUSTRALIAN FOODS

TYPE OF FOOD	OMEGA-6 FATTY ACIDS (G)	OMEGA-3 FATTY ACIDS (G)	LONG CHAIN OMEGA-3 FATTY ACID EQUIVALENT (G)
Margarine, Becel, regular, 1 tbsp (18 g)	8.6	0.05	0.01
Margarine, Becel, light, 1 tbsp (18 g)	4.0	0.04	0.01
Margarine, Flora, regular, 1 tbsp (18 g)	5.8	0.3	0.04
Margarine, Flora light, 1 tbsp (18 g)	3.9	0.1	0.02
Margarine, Gold'n Canola, 1 tbsp (18 g)	2.2	0.9	0.1
Margarine, Gold'n Canola Lifestyle (18 g)	1.7	0.7	0.1
Margarine, polyunsaturated, regular (18 g)	6.3	0.2	0.04
Margarine, polyunsat'd, reduced-fat (18 g)	3.1	0.1	0.02
Margarine, Meadow Lea Poly (18 g)	5.6	0.2	0.02
Margarine, Meadow Lea Canola (18 g)	2.2	1.0	0.1
Margarine, Meadow Lea Lite (18 g)	1.7	0.7	0.1
Margarine, M. Lea Sundew, milk-free (18 g)	2.1	0.9	0.1
Nuttelex, milk-free, 1 tbsp (18 g)	5.8	0.02	0.003
Olive Grove, 1 tbsp (18 g)	2.2	0.4	0.1
Olive oil, 1 tbsp (18 g)	1.8	tr	tr
Palm oil, 1 tbsp (18 g)	1.8	tr	tr
Peanut oil,1 tbsp (18 g)	6.1	0.4	0.05
Safflower oil, 1 tbsp (18 g)	13.9	0.0	0.0
Soybean oil, 1 tbsp (18 g)	9.7	1.4	0.2
Sunflower oil, 1 tbsp (18 g)	11.9	tr	tr
Sunola oil, 1 tbsp (18 g)	1.4	0.0	0.0
Tallow, 1 tbsp (20 g)	0.9	0.0	0.0

POLYUNSATURATED FAT CONTENT OF AUSTRALIAN FOODS

TYPE OF FOOD	OMEGA-6 FATTY ACIDS (G)	OMEGA-3 FATTY ACIDS (G)	LONG CHAIN OMEGA-3 FATTY ACID EQUIVALENT (G)
SALAD DRESSINGS			
Coleslaw dressing, 1 tbsp (20 g)	3.7	0.02	0.003
Coleslaw dressing, reduced-fat (20 g)	1.2	0.02	0.003
French dressing, 1 tbsp (20 g)	2.8	0.1	0.02
Italian dressing, 1 tbsp (20 g)	3.8	0.02	0.003
Mayonnaise, 1 tbsp (30 g)	5.7	0.03	0.005
Mayonnaise, reduced-fat (30 g)	3.7	0.03	0.005
Olive Grove mayonnaise (30 g)	8.7	tr	tr
Praise Caesar dressing, 1 tbsp (20 g)	4.6	tr	tr
Praise, cholesterol-free mayo (30 g)	3.0	tr	tr
Praise, 97% fat-free mayonnaise (30 g)	0.6	tr	tr
Praise French fat-free dressing (20 g)	0.0	0.0	0.0
Praise, light mayonnaise, 1 tbsp (30 g)	5.7	tr	tr
Praise Thousand Island dressing (20 g)	2.8	tr	tr
EGGS			
Egg, whole, raw, 1 egg (48 g edible wt)	0.4	0.05	0.05
Egg, New Start, 1 egg (48 g)	0.4	0.3	0.2
Egg, yolk, chicken, 1 yolk (18 g)	0.6	0.07	0.05
Egg, yolk, duck, 1 yolk (25 g)	0.7	0.2	0.1

POLYUNSATURATED FAT CONTENT OF AUSTRALIAN FOODS

TYPE OF FOOD	OMEGA-6 FATTY ACIDS (G)	OMEGA-3 FATTY ACIDS (G)	LONG CHAIN OMEGA-3 FATTY ACID EQUIVALENT (G)
MILK & DAIRY PRODUCTS			
Brie, 1 wedge (20 g)	0.1	0.06	0.01
Buttermilk, cultured, 1 cup (258 ml)	0.0	0.0	0.0
Cheddar cheese, 1 cube (16 g)	0.08	0.06	0.01
Cottage cheese, 1 tbsp (20 g)	0.04	0.02	0.003
Cottage cheese, low-fat, 1 tbsp (20 g)	0.0	0.0	0.0
Cream, pure, 1 tbsp (18 g)	0.2	0.06	0.01
Cream cheese, 1 tbsp (20 g)	0.1	0.06	0.01
Edam cheese, 1 cube (16 g)	0.06	0.05	0.01
Feta cheese, 1 cube (16 g)	0.06	0.05	0.01
Ricotta cheese, 1 tbsp (20 g)	0.04	0.02	0.003
Swiss cheese, 1 slice (18 g)	0.09	0.05	0.01
Goat's milk, 1 cup (258 ml)	0.3	0.0	0.0
Ice-cream, premium, 1 tbsp (30 g)	0.06	0.03	0.005
Ice-cream, natural, vanilla (27 g)	0.05	0.03	0.005
Milk, low-fat (0.2% fat), 1 cup (259 ml)	0.0	0.0	0.0
Milk, reduced-fat (1.4% fat), 1 cup (260 ml)	0.0	0.0	0.0
Milk, skim (0.1% fat), 1 cup (259 ml)	0.0	0.0	0.0
Milk, full-cream (3.8% fat), 1 cup (258 ml)	0.3	0.0	0.0
Soy milk, So Good™, (3.5% fat), (258 ml)	5.4	0.0	0.0
Soy beverage, unfortified, 1 cup (258 ml)	2.8	0.3	0.04
Sour cream, regular, 1 tbsp (20 g)	0.1	0.06	0.01
Sour cream, light, 1 tbsp (21 g)	0.06	0.04	0.01

POLYUNSATURATED FAT CONTENT OF AUSTRALIAN FOODS

TYPE OF FOOD	OMEGA-6 FATTY ACIDS (G)	OMEGA-3 FATTY ACIDS (G)	LONG CHAIN OMEGA-3 FATTY ACID EQUIVALENT (G)
Yoghurt, fruit, full-fat, 1 tub (200 g)	0.2	0.0	0.0
Yoghurt, fruit, low-fat, 1 tub (200 g)	0.0	0.0	0.0
Yoghurt, natural, full-fat, 1 tub (200 g)	0.2	0.0	0.0
Yoghurt, natural, reduced-fat, 1 tub (200 g)	0.0	0.0	0.0
MEATS			
Beef, lean, 1 steak (145 g) (av)	0.2	0.09	0.06
Chicken breast, no skin, 1 half (79 g)	0.1	0.03	0.03
Chicken paté, 1 slice (35 g) (av)	0.6	0.1	0.04
Kangaroo, lean, 1 small fillet (85 g)	0.2	0.08	0.05
Lamb fillet, lean (59 g)	0.1	0.05	0.03
Lamb kidney, 1 cup sliced (150 g)	0.5	0.3	0.3
Lamb leg steak, lean (65 g)	0.1	0.08	0.05
Ox liver, 1 slice (50 g)	0.4	0.3	0.3
Pork leg steak, raw, lean (82 g)	0.3	0.03	0.02
Sausage, beef, raw, 1 thick (70 g)	0.3	0.1	0.07
Sausage, pork, raw, 1 thick (75 g)	1.3	0.1	0.1
Turkey, no skin, 1 slice (50 g)	0.2	0.02	0.02
Turkey, with skin, 1 slice (55 g)	0.5	0.04	0.02
Turkey loaf, 1 slice (90 g) (av)	0.7	0.05	0.02
FRESH AND CANNED FISH			
Anchovy, canned in oil, drained (5, 18 g)	0.3	0.2	0.1
Barramundi, 1 fillet (150 g) (av)	0.2	0.4	0.4

POLYUNSATURATED FAT CONTENT OF AUSTRALIAN FOODS

TYPE OF FOOD	OMEGA-6 FATTY ACIDS (G)	OMEGA-3 FATTY ACIDS (G)	LONG CHAIN OMEGA-3 FATTY ACID EQUIVALENT (G)
Bream, 1 fillet (150 g) (av)	0.1	0.6	0.6
Cod (1% fat), 1 medium fillet (120 g)	0.1	0.4	0.4
Cod, Antarctic, (4% fat), 1 fillet (120 g)	0.06	0.9	0.9
Crabmeat, canned in brine, drained (145 g)	0.06	0.1	0.1
Dory, John, 1 medium fillet (120 g) (av)	0.04	0.4	0.4
Emperor, 1 fillet (120 g) (av)	0.1	0.3	0.3
Flathead (85 g) (av)	0.1	0.3	0.3
Flounder (100 g) (av)	0.1	0.3	0.2
Garfish (100 g) (av)	0.3	0.6	0.4
Gemfish (175 g) (av)	0.3	1.2	1.1
Jewfish (120 g)	0.05	0.5	0.5
Kingfish (120 g) (av)	0.1	0.6	0.6
Leatherjacket (120 g) (av)	0.1	0.3	0.3
Ling (120 g) (av)	0.04	0.3	0.3
Lobster, cooked, 1 cup pieces (165 g)	0.1	0.3	0.3
Mackerel, fresh (150 g) (av)	0.2	1.2	1.1
Mackerel, canned, 1 cup (190 g) (av)	0.4	4.9	4.0
Mullet (75 g) (av)	0.2	0.7	0.6
Octopus (100 g)	0.03	0.7	0.7
Orange roughy (150 g)	0.3	0.4	0.4
Oyster, Sydney rock, 12 raw (60 g)	0.1	0.8	0.6
Perch (120 g) (av)	0.2	0.5	0.4
Prawn, king, 5 cooked (80 g)	0.05	0.1	0.1

POLYUNSATURATED FAT CONTENT OF AUSTRALIAN FOODS

TYPE OF FOOD	OMEGA-6 FATTY ACIDS (G)	OMEGA-3 FATTY ACIDS (G)	LONG CHAIN OMEGA-3 FATTY ACID EQUIVALENT (G)
Rock-cod, yellow-spotted (95 g)	0.2	0.6	0.6
Salmon, Atlantic (150 g)	0.9	3.2	2.8
Salmon, Australian (150 g) (av)	0.2	0.9	0.9
Salmon, Australian, canned, 1 cup (210 g)	0.2	2.3	2.1
Salmon, pink, canned, 1 cup (210 g) (av)	0.2	3.1	2.8
Salmon, red, canned, 1 cup (210 g) (av)	0.3	3.7	3.2
Sardine, canned, 5 sardines (80 g) (av)	1.6	2.4	2.1
Scallop, 1 cup heated (160 g)	0.03	0.2	0.2
Sea-perch (100 g) (av)	0.1	0.4	0.4
Shark (150 g) (av)	0.1	0.4	0.4
Skate (150 g) (av)	0.1	0.5	0.5
Snapper (105 g) (av)	0.1	0.4	0.4
Squid, 1 cup (95 g)	0.03	0.4	0.4
Sweetlips, painted (150 g)	0.3	0.5	0.4
Tailor, with skin (150 g)	0.4	2.3	2.0
Trevally (150 g) (av)	0.2	0.4	0.4
Trout, rainbow (120 g) (av)	0.4	0.7	0.6
Tuna, southern bluefin, with skin (150 g)	0.3	1.7	1.6
Tuna, canned in brine, 1 cup (190 g)	0.1	1.3	1.2
Whiting, 1 fillet (55 g) (av)	0.1	0.2	0.2

TYPE OF FOOD	OMEGA-6 FATTY ACIDS (G)	OMEGA-3 FATTY ACIDS (G)	LONG CHAIN OMEGA-3 FATTY ACID EQUIVALENT (G)
NUTS AND SEEDS			
Almond, ½ cup (83 g) (av)	10.8	0.0	0.0
Brazil nut, ½ cup (85 g)	2.5	0.0	0.0
Cashew, ½ cup (75 g) (av)	5.7	0.0	0.0
Coconut, dessicated, 1 cup (75 g)	0.5	0.0	0.0
Coconut, fresh, 3 large pieces (75 g)	0.2	0.0	0.0
Coconut cream, 1 cup (290 g)	0.6	0.0	0.0
Hazelnut, ½ cup (70 g)	4.9	0.1	0.01
Macadamia, ½ cup (73 g)	0.7	0.0	0.0
Marzipan, ¼ roll (50 g)	2.0	0.0	0.0
Nuts, mixed, salted, ½ cup (75 g)	11.3	0.0	0.0
Peanuts with skin, ½ cup (78 g) (av)	12.2	0.0	0.0
Peanut butter, 1 tbsp (25 g) (av)	4.1	0.0	0.0
Pecan, ½ cup (55 g)	13.3	0.3	0.05
Pine nut, 1 tbsp (14 g)	5.6	0.0	0.0
Pistachio, ½ cup (63 g)	10.0	0.0	0.0
Sesame seed, 1 tbsp (13 g)	3.2	0.0	0.0
Sunflower seed, 1 tbsp (16 g)	5.5	0.0	0.0
Tahini paste, 1 tbsp (20 g)	5.6	0.02	0.003
Walnut, ½ cup, chopped (55 g)	23.8	3.5	0.5

The figures in this table are based on data for 100 gram portions listed in the following reference: Meyer, B. J., Tsivis, E., Howe, P. R. C., Tapsell, L. & Calvert, G. D., 'Polyunsaturated Fatty Acid Content of Foods: Differentiating Between Long and Short Chain Omega-3 Fatty Acids', *Food Australia*, vol. 51, pp.81–95, 1999.

Chapter 4

The Benefits of Mediterranean-style Diets

The main problem with nutrition in industrialised nations is over-nutrition—too much food for our sedentary lifestyles and a predominance of foods that have been linked to cardiovascular disease or overweight. Because fat contains the most energy per gram and is less satiating than carbohydrate or protein, most experts consider that high fat diets are the cause of overweight and its disease consequences. Dietary guidelines in Australia and other developed countries therefore emphasise the importance of eating a low fat diet. Fat, irrespective of type, has become the dietary 'villain'. However, we now know that this is an over-simplification and that some types of diets are healthy diets despite their high fat content.

In the 1980s, scientists were surprised to learn that the rates of heart disease and cancer in parts of Greece where the traditional dietary patterns were maintained were low in contrast to the rates in Australia, Europe and North America.

Controlled trials since then have shown the favourable effects of a Mediterranean-style diet on cholesterol, blood pressure and therefore risk of heart disease. The Lyon Heart Study (see page 34) mimicked aspects of a Mediterranean-style diet by increasing intakes of vegetables, fruits, fish and olive oil (which together supply vitamins such as folic acid, vitamin B6, carotenoids and tocopherols and monounsaturated and omega-3 fatty acids) and showed a reduction in death from coronary heart disease. The Mediterranean diet is considered beneficial not only because of lower saturated and high monounsaturated fats, but because it is rich in micronutrients that act by a variety of mechanisms to reduce the risk of heart disease.

The Seven Countries Study

The classic Seven Countries Study, led by Ancel Keys, demonstrated that countries in which saturated fat intake was low, such as Japan and rural Mediterranean areas in southern Europe, had much lower rates of coronary disease than the United States and northern Europe where saturated fat intake was high. There was no relationship, however, between total fat intake and coronary disease; that is, high total fat intake did not mean increased disease risk. This is because Mediterranean diets are not only low in saturated fat but high in olive oil, which is rich in **monounsaturated fatty acids (MUFA)** and accounted for the high total fat intake. In addition, Mediterranean diets are rich in fruits and vegetables containing potentially protective nutrients called phytochemicals.

The lowest rate of coronary disease was in Crete, which has the highest intake of total fat—nearly all from olive oil. Japan also has very low coronary rates, coinciding with low total fat intake. Thus Japan and Crete could be considered two models of healthy eating: one based on rice, soy and fish and low in fat, the other based on cereals, vegetables, fish and olive oil and high in fat. A 25-year follow-up of the Seven Countries cohorts continued to show very low rates of heart disease in Japan and rural areas of southern Europe. Cancer rates, particularly of those cancers whose rates are high in northern Europe, the United States and Australia (colon, prostate and breast), are low in Crete as well as in Japan.

PASTA

AVERAGE GI 40

Most pasta is made from semolina (finely cracked wheat) which is milled from very hard wheat with a high protein content. Durum wheat is a high protein wheat considered to make the best pasta. A stiff dough, made by mixing the semolina with water, is forced through a die and dried. There is minimal mechanical disruption of the starch granule during this process and strong protein–starch interactions inhibit starch gelatinisation. The dense consistency also makes the pasta resistant to disruption in the small intestine and contributes to the final low GI—even pasta made from fine flour instead of semolina has a relatively low GI. There is some evidence that thicker pasta has a lower GI than thin types for this reason. The addition of egg to fresh pasta lowers the GI by increasing the protein content. Higher protein levels slow stomach emptying.

Why are Mediterranean-style diets good for us?

The low coronary rates recorded by people on Mediterranean diets are likely to come from the favourable effect the diet has on cholesterol concentrations in the blood. Many studies have shown that reducing intake of saturated fat and replacing it with either carbohydrates or unsaturated oils lowers blood concentrations of LDL cholesterol—a firmly established cause of hardening of the arteries. However, replacing saturated fats with carbohydrate can also lower HDL cholesterol, which protects against cholesterol accumulation in artery walls. Lower HDL concentrations are associated with higher coronary rates. But monounsaturated fats do not have this HDL-lowering action. In the Lyon Heart Study, the high carbohydrate diet, but not the monounsaturated diet, increased blood triglycerides, another coronary risk factor. Taken together, a high carbohydrate–low fat diet had a mixed effect on blood lipids whereas high monounsaturated fat diets had only beneficial effects.

Some of the micronutrients in Mediterranean-style diets may act to reduce disease by mechanisms other than improving blood fats. One of these micronutrients is folate, which is found in organ meats and green leafy vegetables. This vitamin is in short supply in many diets, and relative deficiency has been found to result in high levels of an amino acid called 'homocysteine' in the blood. Diets rich in folate result in lower levels of homocysteine in the blood. Although we don't know why or how, high levels of homocysteine are associated with a high risk of heart disease. Diets high in fruit and vegetables also provide antioxidants that protect blood lipids and other compounds from oxidation. Oxidised cholesterol fractions in the blood are more likely to lead to hardened arteries.

High blood pressure or hypertension is another risk factor for cardiovascular incidents such as heart attack and stroke. High intake of vegetable products is associated with lower blood pressure levels and low stroke rate worldwide. The DASH (Dietary Approaches to Stop Hypertension) study found that increased intake of fruits, vegetables and nuts reduced blood pressure. In fact, the results in mildly hypertensive patients were astounding, far exceeding the results of other non-pharmacological interventions (such as low salt diets) and similar to drug therapy. In Italy, Mediterranean-style diets in a research setting have also lowered blood pressure.

A low fat diet or a Mediterranean diet?

You may be wondering why we continue to encourage a high carbohydrate diet when there is so much to recommend the lower carbohydrate Mediterranean-style diet. Well, the high carbohydrate diets used for comparison in research studies with Mediterranean-style diets were invariably based on high glycemic index carbohydrate foods, even though the researchers were at pains to stress high intake of starch and fibre (that is, complex carbohydrate). Readers of *The Glucose Revolution* will already know that most of the common starchy foods in Western diets, including wholemeal breads, flours and potatoes, have a high glycemic index.

We believe one of the reasons for the success of Mediterranean-style diets is

because they reduce the intake of high glycemic index foods, thereby reducing glucose and insulin responses. In crossover studies, high carbohydrate diets in which the foods were based on low glycemic index foods (such as pasta and legumes) produced altogether favourable (not mixed) effects on blood lipids. That is, the low GI diets, compared with the high GI diets, improved triglyceride levels and did not lower HDL levels (the two main concerns with high carbohydrate diets). In one study comparing high and low GI diets with a high MUFA diet, HDL actually increased on the low GI diet and did not change on the high MUFA diet. In a large study of 2000 healthy adults in Britain, HDL levels were correlated best not with the type of fat but with the glycemic index of the diet: the lower the glycemic index, the higher the HDL level.

There is a widening divide in the nutrition and public health community between those who advocate a low fat diet and those who promote a Mediterranean-style diet. This has led to conflicting information and understandable confusion. Our view is that the optimal diet can be low fat **or** Mediterranean-style—the priority is to lower both saturated fat and high glycemic index carbohydrate in both cases. Which type of diet you choose is an individual decision that will be influenced by your lifestyle, ethnic origins, weight and activity level. Judging from the very low incidence in the Mediterranean and parts of Asia of cardiovascular disease and the cancers that plague our society, both traditional dietary patterns have the potential to dramatically benefit our population.

It is understandable that people of Asian origin may choose a high rice diet while people of southern European origin might choose the Mediterranean diet. An overweight individual of Anglo-Celtic origin might benefit most from a high carbohydrate diet based on low glycemic index foods—it will be bulkier and more satiating than a more energy-dense high MUFA diet. If you are very physically active, the high MUFA diet will help you to eat sufficient energy without compromising nutrition. Mediterranean-style diets should still be bulky—it depends on how you combine foods in your high MUFA diet. If you simply exchange saturated fat for olive oil in cooking and in margarines, chances are the diet will still be very energy dense and easy to 'passively overconsume'. It's important to recognise that there is more to the Mediterranean diet than olive oil!

Dietary recommendations for diabetes: high or low carbohydrate?

There is concern in some quarters that high carbohydrate diets are especially deleterious for people with diabetes and some experts recommend high fat, high MUFA diets instead. Is this advice justified? The aim of dietary management of diabetes is to normalise blood glucose and blood lipid levels in order to prevent the short- and long-term complications of diabetes, particularly coronary heart disease. People with diabetes are 3 to 4 times more likely to die of a heart attack than people without diabetes, even when cholesterol levels and blood pressure are the same. For this reason, dietary recommendations for diabetes have long emphasised reducing saturated fat. However, if saturated fat intake is reduced, the energy has to be replaced by some other nutrient. Protein, carbohydrate, PUFA or MUFA: which is it to be?

High protein diets

At present, a very high protein intake is not recommended for people with diabetes because it might increase the rate of progression of kidney problems (chronic renal failure). Most people with diabetes are at increased risk of developing kidney disease because high blood glucose levels put stress on the kidney's filtering mechanisms. The kidney's job is to filter waste products but salvage nutrients from the blood—it retains the sugars in the blood as best it can but if blood glucose levels are higher than about 10 millimoles, the kidney can't cope and the excess sugars are lost into the urine. The presence of glucose in the urine is often the way that diabetes is first diagnosed. If kidney function has deteriorated because of the excess glucose in the urine, the added stress of filtering the waste products of a high protein diet might be the straw that breaks the camel's back. For this reason, some experts recommend low protein diets for people with renal complications of diabetes. However, in early diabetes without renal complications, there is no strong evidence that a low protein diet is advantageous.

In people without diabetes and with healthy kidneys, there may be advantages to a higher protein intake which we describe in Chapter 6. In theory, these advantages would also apply to people with diabetes and healthy kidneys. Researchers in Melbourne studied four different diets for four weeks in people with diabetes, in an attempt to determine which type was associated with the best diabetes control. To their surprise, the very high protein diet containing over 60 per cent energy as protein (and less fat and carbohydrate than people normally eat) gave the best control: lower glucose and insulin levels, lower blood cholesterol, better glucose tolerance. The next best diet was the high carbohydrate, high fibre one that is currently recommended for people with diabetes. The researchers concluded that the latter was the most practical for most people because the high protein diet was not easy to eat, was expensive, and was not environmentally sound. Although some of these criticisms are arguable, it is probably true that most people would find it hard to stick to a diet where over 50 per cent of the energy comes from protein.

High MUFA diets

The main controversy is centred on whether saturated fat energy should be replaced with carbohydrate or MUFA. In the United States, the current nutritional recommendations for people with diabetes indicate that carbohydrate and MUFA can be considered interchangeable, and the proportions determined by individual needs and desires. They argue in favour of allowing higher MUFA intake on the grounds that high carbohydrate diets can increase blood glucose and insulin concentrations and result in high triglycerides and low HDL levels in the blood—changes that are atherogenic and increase the risk of coronary heart disease.

We think it might be too soon to wholeheartedly recommend a Western diet based on high MUFA. Why? Firstly, the American Diabetes Association doesn't consider the source of the carbohydrate (that is, its glycemic index) when discussing high carbohydrate diets. Many dietary trials have shown that lowering the GI of dietary carbohydrate (with no change in total amount) improves blood glucose control, as assessed by glycated haemoglobin (HbA1c) or fructosamine, by an average of 10 per cent. The magnitude of this effect is the same as we see when type 2 diabetes is treated with oral hypoglycemic drugs or with insulin.

Secondly, while high MUFA diets reduce post-meal glucose and insulin responses (because each meal contains less carbohydrate), there is no evidence that they improve overall glycemic control as assessed by HbA1c. This contrasts with the consistent effect of high carbohydrate, low GI diets in lowering HbA1c.

Thirdly, the clearly positive effects of high MUFA diets on blood lipids are seen only when the high MUFA diet is extremely high in fat (as much as 45 to 50 per cent of energy) and very low in carbohydrate (about 35 per cent of energy). In studies with smaller and more realistic dietary changes, the effects of MUFA on blood lipids are quite modest. Very high fat diets may promote insulin resistance and weight gain. Furthermore, the effects of MUFA on triglycerides have been shown in subjects with normal triglycerides, not diabetes patients with high triglycerides. It is not logical to extrapolate from one to the other.

MUFA may be useful nonetheless in the treatment of high blood lipids in people with diabetes in the context of a low fat diet. Thus a diet containing 30 per cent energy from fat with a high proportion of MUFA has been found to produce modest improvements in HDL and triglycerides.

Very high fat diets may promote weight gain

Several studies lately have suggested that high MUFA diets are as effective as high carbohydrate diets in producing weight loss. However, in these studies, MUFA were used in the context of a strictly controlled low energy diet. The long-term effect of Western diets enriched in MUFA on body weight regulation is currently anybody's guess. This is an important issue because weight loss is a primary aim in the treatment of most people with type 2 diabetes. There is concern that the promotion of increased MUFA may result in high overall energy intake, which may prevent weight loss or promote weight gain. Many studies (but not all!) suggest that the prevalence of obesity in both men and women is higher in people with high fat intakes (expressed as a percentage of energy) than in those with low fat intakes. In addition, there is good evidence that reducing fat intake with ad libitum intake of carbohydrate is the most successful strategy in promoting long-term weight loss.

Why should a high fat diet promote weight gain? Several theories have been put forward. Jean-Pierre Flatt, for example, has pointed out that the body can use fat, carbohydrate or protein as a fuel and that in a steady state (weight balance), the amount of each fuel burnt must be equal to the proportions of these nutrients provided in diet. He suggested that fat is fattening because the body has a very limited ability to store protein and carbohydrate but a very large capacity to store fat. So protein and carbohydrate in the diet are preferentially burnt and dietary fat is preferentially stored. Every day we will burn virtually all the carbohydrate and protein we ingest. We will only burn fat when it is released from the fat stores or the liver as 'free fatty acids'.

In fact, the level of free fatty acids in our bloodstream directly influences the level of fat burning: the higher the level of free fatty acids, the higher the rate of fat burning. So what determines the level of

free fatty acids in the blood? Studies show that this relates directly to the amount of fat stored. In a steady state of weight balance the amount of fat burnt each day must equal the amount provided in the diet. If the amount of fat provided in the diet is high, body fat stores *must* expand to make the level of free fatty acids in the blood correspond. So a high fat diet brings about a high fat body.

The combination of high fat and high glycemic index carbohydrate may be a particularly fattening combination. This is because the high insulin response induced by the carbohydrate tells the body to burn **more** carbohydrate and **less** fat. In fact, one of insulin's most powerful actions is to switch off the release of free fatty acids from the fat stores. So dietary fat will tend to be stored and remain in store rather than burned while insulin levels are raised.

Unfortunately, many of us have chronically high insulin levels because we are 'insulin resistant': that is, our body resists the normal actions of insulin. To overcome this insulin resistance, the body produces more and more insulin to move the glucose out of the bloodstream and into the muscles, where it is burnt. Over the course of the day, insulin levels are raised with the net effect of burning more carbohydrate and less fat. We believe this encourages increasing fat storage over the course of time. Compounding the problem, carbohydrate stores in the body are thought to act as a hunger barometer: when stores are low we feel hungry, when they are full we feel satiated. But if carbohydrate stores are fluctuating widely throughout the day under the influence of insulin, the net effect may be a slight excess intake of energy; that is, gradual weight gain.

There are other reasons why high fat diets might encourage weight gain. In one study, when investigators covertly increased dietary fat from 20 per cent to 60 per cent of energy, the subjects overate—kilojoules in exceeded kilojoules out—and stored extra fat. In another study, students ate as much as they liked from a palatable smorgasbord of foods—on one occasion the foods were all high in carbohydrate and on another they were all high in fat. The students were 'blind' to the nutrient content of the foods and the true purpose of the study. The investigators found that the students unconsciously ate almost twice as many kilojoules from the smorgasbord of high fat foods.

In another study, volunteers were given either a high carbohydrate snack or a high fat snack and one hour later allowed to eat from an array of palatable foods. They ate significantly more when the earlier snack was high in fat.

As a result of studies such as these, scientists now say that fat is very easy to 'passively overconsume'. We believe it is one of the most important and robust findings in nutrition science over the past decade. It has turned upside down the general belief that fat is particularly satiating. The opposite is true! Of course a high fat meal can make you feel full, even biliously full. But the point is that you will have eaten an excessively large number of kilojoules before you register your fullness. We all recognise how easy it is to demolish a plate of chips or peanuts.

A word about low fat foods

It's generally true to say that a high fat food is more energy dense (that is, has more kilojoules per gram) than a low fat, high carbohydrate food; for example, peanuts contain 2300 kilojoules per 100 grams, while jellybeans contain only 400 kilojoules per 100 grams. But it is not always true—and it's becoming increasingly common to find low fat foods on the market that are as energy-dense as their full fat counterparts.

For example, some low fat flavoured yoghurts contain 440 kilojoules per 100 grams compared with 400 kilojoules per 100 grams for the full fat counterpart. This is because the low fat yoghurt contains extra carbohydrate to create a creamy texture. The added carbohydrate compensates for the reduction in fat, both texture-wise and kilojoule-wise! So it's not always true to say that high carbohydrate foods are bulky and satiating. In addition, it has been suggested that when people see the words 'low fat' on a food label, they interpret this as a licence to eat more and so may consume twice as many kilojoules. This phenomenon may partly explain why the prevalence of obesity continues to increase in countries like the United States, Canada and Australia, despite evidence of reduced fat intake.

Realistic dietary prescriptions

The American Diabetes Association remains quite adamant that the amount of carbohydrate consumed is more important in the management of diabetes than the type of carbohydrate. (This applies to both the low versus high GI distinction, as well as the starch versus sugar distinction.) But what happens in practice when we advise people to eat specified amounts of carbohydrate and fat? In one study, over 70 subjects with type 2 diabetes were randomly selected to receive advice to follow one of three types of diets: weight reducing, high MUFA or high carbohydrate. After 18 months, the investigators found no differences in body weight, diet composition or blood glucose and lipid

control! In contrast, a study from Hammersmith Hospital in London showed that advice which focused on the *type* of carbohydrate (that is, glycemic index) resulted in higher fibre intake and lower saturated fat intake, and improved both blood glucose and blood cholesterol in comparison with standard dietary advice based on the amount of carbohydrate.

Other health concerns

A large increase in MUFA intake, such that total energy as fat is above 35 per cent, may produce improvements in triglyceride levels and HDL but it is not consistent with dietary guidelines for the public, nor with dietary guidelines to prevent cancer and heart disease. It should not be forgotten that modifying the source of carbohydrate, for example by using low GI foods, can have the same beneficial effect as MUFA. Low GI diets have none of the potential problems of increased fat intake.

The last word

The Mediterranean diet contains lots of carbohydrates that have a low glycemic index—pasta, beans and fruit in particular—and meals are often eaten with a salad and vinaigrette which we know also lowers the glycemic impact of a meal. The potentially high GI of white bread in the diet would be reduced by the fact that it is eaten with low GI foods.

As long as total fat intake is not too high (that is, no more than 30–35 per cent of energy), Mediterranean-style diets are likely to benefit people with diabetes. Compare the GI values of common carbohydrate foods in Western versus Mediterranean diets (below).

WESTERN DIET	GI	MEDITERRANEAN DIET	GI
WHITE BREAD	70	WHITE BREAD	70
POTATO	80–100	PASTA	40
BREAKFAST CEREAL	70–80	LEGUMES	20–30
BISCUITS	60–70	FRUIT	30-40

THE TAKE-HOME MESSAGE

■ Mediterranean-style diets, despite their high fat content, have proven health benefits.

■ Mediterranean-style diets are more than just a lot of olive oil.

■ Choose legumes, pasta, salad vegetables and vinegar dressings as an integral part of your Mediterranean-style diet.

■ A Mediterranean-style diet is suitable for people with diabetes who do not have a weight problem.

■ A high protein–low fat diet is best avoided by people with diabetes until we know more about its effects on renal function.

Adapting our diet to the Mediterranean way of eating

The Mediterranean diet contains an abundance of plant foods including vegetables, fruits and legumes. Olive oil is part of the daily diet, and fish is eaten more frequently than red meat. Because alcoholic beverages are seen as a traditional part of meals in the Mediterranean, a glass of red wine has been included with the main meal.

This style of diet reflects current dietary recommendations where the emphasis on eating low fat is relaxed in favour of including more mono-unsaturated fats. Most of the carbohydrate is of a low GI.

Suggested quantities of each food have been included. The menu provides 8400 kilojoules/2000 calories, with approximately 15 per cent of energy from protein, 35 per cent from fat and 45 per cent from carbo-hydrate. The P:M:S ratio is approximately 1:5:2.

BREAKFAST

Bread with feta cheese and olives	2 slices of white bread with 50 g of feta cheese and 6 olives
Coffee and fresh fruit	1 cup of coffee and 2 fresh peaches

MIDDAY MEAL

Pasta with tomato sauce	1 cup of cooked pasta with 100 g tomato sauce
Green bean, rocket and tomato salad with vinaigrette	Standard serving
Bread with avocado and olive oil	1 slice of bread, ¼ avocado and drizzle of olive oil
Fresh fruit	200 g fresh cherries

EVENING MEAL

Chargrilled blue-eye cod with borlotti beans	120 g fish cutlet with 80 g borlotti beans
Roast capsicum, sweet potato and herb salad	Red capsicum, 150 g sweet potato, parsley, chives
Bread and lettuce with vinaigrette	1 slice of bread with mixed lettuce and 1 tablespoon of vinaigrette
Fruit and nuts	1 cup of black grapes, 1 dried fig, 3 almonds
Red wine	1 glass
Coffee	1 cup

Chapter 5

The Benefits
of Asian-style Diets

People living traditionally throughout Asia have low rates of heart disease, type 2 diabetes and cancer. One of the obvious reasons is that they do not become overweight or obese as they age. This might have as much to do with lifestyle factors such as physical activity and food availability as with diet. Nonetheless, their diet is different to that of the rest of the world and proves the point that high carbohydrate diets are commensurate with good health. Asian-style diets are characterised by rice; it is the staple food consumed in large amounts at all meals. It is usually white rice, and the variety and characteristics of the rice are of utmost importance, and different for different population groups. Along with the rice goes small amounts of animal food (poultry, fish) and varying amounts of vegetables and fruits. In India, mashed legumes, called dhals, are a common accompaniment with a proven low glycemic index. Traditional Asian-style diets are invariably low in fat, although they may be relatively rich in omega-3 fats. Japanese people, for example, regularly eat fish and seaweed, both good sources of omega-3 fats.

There are other benefits to Asian-style diets. Because meat and fish are expensive commodities, large amounts of soybean and other vegetables accompany the rice, including, in Japan and Korea, seaweed. From a health perspective, it is this aspect which may be the most important component of the Asian diet. The vegetable component increases the intake of micronutrients such as antioxidants, vitamins, minerals, and phytochemicals such as isoflavones and phytoestrogens.

The benefits of high fruit and vegetable intake

Five million years ago, the ancestors of the first hominids lived in the rainforests of Africa. Their diet was based on fruits, nuts, berries and insects and supplemented with animal food. Although the tables turned and animal food began to dominate as humans evolved, we have inherited the requirements for a substantial intake of the substances found in fruit and vegetables. In fact, there is overwhelming evidence for fruit and vegetables playing a role in disease prevention, especially cancer prevention. The evidence is more consistently linked to vegetable consumption and is stronger for raw rather than cooked foods. Of course, it's possible that a high fruit and vegetable intake is an indicator of an overall healthy lifestyle, including plenty of physical activity and the avoidance of smoking and drugs. Canadian Inuit (Eskimos) got by with very little in the way of fresh fruit and vegetables, but they also ate the organs of animals and fish and thereby procured many of the same substances found in fruit and vegetables. Unfortunately, however, most of us these days don't eat organ meat or offal very often.

Scientists have tried to pinpoint the protective factors in vegetables. The most obvious candidates were the orange pigment compounds called carotenoids (because they were originally detected in carrots) which are found in all yellow, orange and dark green fruits and vegetables. However, when pure carotenes were tested as supplements, there was no protective effect and possibly a harmful effect. There are many other candidates: vitamin C, vitamin E, selenium, dietary fibre, flavonoids, phenols, plant sterols and protease inhibitors—any or all of these may be the substances in fruit and vegetables which give the protective effects.

How do these protective factors work? Possibly, by binding and diluting carcinogenic substances in the gut, by antioxidant effects, by the induction of detoxifying enzymes, by inhibiting the formation of nitrosamines and by alterating the metabolism of hormones. It's more than likely that it is the combined effect of these substances that is responsible, rather than any one component. So don't be tempted to take a multivitamin supplement to replace a high intake of fruit and vegetables—you won't find all of the protective substances in a pill.

ASIAN-STYLE DRESSING

Combine 1 tablespoon each of canola oil and lemon or lime juice with 1 teaspoon each of sesame oil and soy sauce. Add a clove of crushed garlic and 1 small finely minced chilli. Serve with grilled meat or fish and mixed leaf salad or finely shredded cabbage.

Avoiding cancer

In the United Kingdom, a major report on diet and cancer found no evidence for any specific food causing cancer. However, they concluded that high intakes of vegetables, fruit and cereal products seemed to protect against cancers at all sites. On the basis of the best evidence available at the time (1998), these experts made the following recommendations to avoid cancer:

- Maintain a healthy body weight throughout adulthood
- Eat more fruit and vegetables
- Eat more dietary fibre
- Limit intake of red and processed meat to 5 to 8 serves per week
- Avoid high doses of vitamin and mineral supplements

In Australia, the experts believe that there is no association between red meat consumption and cancer. Australian meat is very different from that in Europe and North America because it is leaner with much less saturated fat. They do recommend, however, that meat eaters should avoid charred meat and deep browning of meat surfaces. So when you're barbecuing:

- Cook meat more gently
- Choose rare over well done
- Don't allow the flame to come in contact with the meat

The benefits of soy

Many studies suggest that soybeans, and products made from them, such as tofu, protect Japanese, Chinese and other Asian populations from developing the high rates of heart disease and breast cancer that normally plague Western populations. In many Asian countries, soy is a staple food and is used in many forms, including soy milk, soy sauce, soy flour. One explanation for the findings is that soy helps to reduce high blood lipid levels. We like to think that the slow digestion and absorption of the carbohydrate in soybeans might also have something to do with it, although others believe the protein fraction is responsible.

Some studies suggest that the isoflavones in soybeans are responsible for reducing the risk of breast cancer.

These substances are thought to antagonise the action of the hormone oestrogen in pre-menopausal women. Western women, especially overweight ones, are thought to produce too much oestrogen, thereby stimulating the growth of abnormal breast tissue. Soy products are one of the best dietary sources of these isoflavones—or phytoestrogens as they are often called. During and after menopause, the isoflavones are believed to reduce hot flushes and other symptoms characteristic of this stage. However, we still have quite a way to go to prove all this.

In the meantime, we know that soybeans have one of the lowest GI values of any food. Their addition to main meals and salads helps to reduce the overall GI of the diet.

AVERAGE GI 18

Soybeans and soy products have been a staple part of Asian diets for thousands of years. We have traditionally known soybeans as an excellent source of protein and as very rich in fibre, iron, zinc and vitamin B. They are lower in carbohydrate and higher in fat than other legumes but the majority of the fat is polyunsaturated. Soybeans can contribute beneficial amounts of the plant form of omega-3 fat (alpha linolenic acid, or ALA) to your diet, with just ¼ cup of soybeans containing 0.5 grams of ALA.

More recently, soy has been recognised as a rich source of natural plant chemicals called phytochemicals, and in particular phytoestrogens. Phytoestrogens are a plant oestrogen with a structure similar to the female hormone oestrogen, but with a much weaker action. The specific phytoestrogens in soy are known as isoflavones and the two main types are genistein and daidzein. There are many studies associating these components of soy with health benefits that include improvements in blood cholesterol levels, alleviation of menopausal symptoms and lowered rates of cancer.

Two to three daily serves of soy are believed to be necessary to achieve optimum benefit. There are various ways to incorporate soy into your diet:

Soybeans, which can be purchased canned, can be used in any recipe in place of other beans.

Soy can be consumed in a drink, such as So Good™.

Firm tofu can be simply cut into cubes, marinated (try soy sauce, ginger and garlic) and added to stir-fries or threaded onto kebabs for the barbecue.

Silken tofu can be used as a base for cheesecakes, creamy sauces and salad dressings.

Soy flour can be substituted for half a cup of wheat flour in baked goods.

Soy grits can be incorporated into homemade bread to lower its GI.

Which type of rice should you eat?

Because rice is the dominating carbohydrate source in Asian diets, its glycemic index determines to a large degree the overall glycemic index of the Asian-style eating pattern. As readers of *The New Glucose Revolution* will already be aware, rice varies markedly in its GI depending on the variety. Most Australian rices, such as Calrose, have a high GI, while Basmati rice from India and the rice eaten in Japan have a low GI. The reason for the variation is the type of starch present. Those varieties with more amylose-type starch have a lower GI. Amylose is a straight-chain starch molecule that tends to line up with itself in rows, forming tight bonds that make it difficult to

gelatinise (expand with water) during cooking. Amylose starch needs higher temperatures and longer cooking times in order to gelatinise compared with the branched-chain starch called amylopectin. Because the starch isn't fully gelatinised in cooking, the higher amylose rice has a lower GI.

Some rices, such as glutinous rice or sticky rice, contain only amylopectin with no amylose at all. As a result, the texture of the rice is quite different—all the starch molecules are gelatinised, and some have escaped the confines of the starch granule. The individual grains of rice stick to each other, hence the name sticky rice. On the other hand, rices with a high amylose content retain more of their starch in the ungelatinised form, and the grains maintain greater individual integrity: you can pick up individual grains of rice. Many varieties of rice have an intermediate amount of amylose and the rice has a moderate level of stickiness.

To many people in Asia and to the other rice connoisseurs of the world, these subtle characteristics are of utmost importance—they will reject rice that does not meet their usual expectations. This is one reason that Australian rice growers have had difficulties exporting their rice: most varieties of Australian rice tend to be low in amylose and have a high GI. In contrast, many Asian varieties have a high amylose or intermediate amylose content and a lower GI.

PRODUCT	GI	COMMENT
Basmati rice	58	Long grain rice with aromatic flavour that develops with storage. Higher amylose content (35 per cent of the starch is amylose) compared to other rices, which accounts for its lower GI
Doongara rice	56	Long grain Australian-grown high amylose (28 per cent) rice which is more slowly digested than other Australian rices
Parboiled rice, e.g. Jasmine	109	Parboiling of rice involves steeping paddy rice in hot water then steaming, drying and milling it. This process retains extra nutrients in the starchy endosperm of the grain but does not affect the GI
Short grain Australian rice, e.g. Calrose and Pelde (brown & white)	80	Normal Australian rices that contain 20 per cent of their starch as amylose and have high GI values
Short grain Japanese rice	48	This short grain rice, which is eaten by people every day in Japan, has a low GI despite an amylose content of only 20 per cent
Waxy rice (0–2 per cent amylose)	88	Sticky type of rice used in rice desserts. Has a very high GI probably due to the absence of amylose starch

PRODUCT	GI	COMMENT
Vermicelli	35	A thinner version of spaghetti that cooks quickly and is good to add to soups and stir-fries
Tortellini/Ravioli	45	Two different shapes of filled pasta. Buy fresh or vacuum packed, boil and serve with a pasta sauce. The fat content will vary depending on the filling and the sauce
Spaghetti	38	Like all pasta, spaghetti has a low GI because it is made from high protein semolina and has a dense food matrix that resists disruption in the small intestine
Lungkow bean thread noodles	26	Also known as cellophane noodles or green bean vermicelli, these shiny fine white noodles are made from mung beans. Their low GI is attributable to their legume origin and noodle shape. Soak in hot water then add to stir-fries and salads. Look for them in Asian supermarkets
Instant noodles	46	A popular meal or snack these days, but many types are high in fat. The flavour sachets are based on salt and monosodium glutamate. Plain, quick-cooking wheat or rice noodles are a healthier alternative

Adapting our diet to the Asian way of eating

Asian-style diets differ from Western diets in many ways, one of which is the proportion of plant to animal foods. In this menu, although the protein content is similar to that of many Western diets at 15 per cent of energy, more of it is of plant origin than animal origin. The carbohydrate content is high due to the staple of rice and noodles.

Suggested quantities of each food have been included. This menu supplies 8400 kilojoules/2000 calories, with 15 per cent of energy from protein, 25 per cent of energy from fat and 55 per cent of energy from carbohydrate. The P:M:S ratio is approximately 2:2:1.

BREAKFAST

Noodles in stock with green vegetable and tofu	85 g wheat noodles with chicken stock, spring onion, Chinese spinach and 50 g tofu

SNACK

Fresh fruit	1 apple

MIDDAY MEAL

Boiled rice with a stir-fried vegetable and fried fish	2 cups of cooked rice with a bunch of choy sum, onion, soy sauce and 65 g fish fried in peanut oil

SNACK

Soy drink and fresh fruit	Soy drink and 2 fresh apricots

EVENING MEAL

Chicken vermicelli soup	Standard serve of chicken vermicelli soup
Stir-fried vegetable and pork belly with boiled rice	1 cup of cooked rice with 25 g pork belly and 2 cups of Chinese greens
Fresh fruit	Standard serve of fresh fruit salad

SNACK

Small serve of nuts	Handful of almonds

Chapter 6

Paleolithic Nutrition: the High Protein Diet

Humans have come a long way since prehistoric days of hunting and gathering. Almost everything has changed, including our diet. But one thing has remained basically unaltered: our genes. About 99 per cent of our genetic make-up was defined long before our forebears evolved into Homo sapiens (literally, 'wise man') 50 000 years ago. Scientists believe that one species of chimpanzee began the gradual process of evolution into modern human beings about seven million years ago. The first hominids (human-like creatures) walked upright about four million years ago. Significantly, around 2.5 million years ago the climate in Africa and elsewhere began to cool down, giving rise to the first of a long series of ice ages. Rainforests eventually gave way to savanna; grassland became the dominant vegetation. In this new climate, herbivorous animals proliferated, as did carnivorous creatures that preyed upon them.

The last two million years of human evolution have occurred against a backdrop of ice ages, spiked by short warmer inter-glacial periods, such as the current one. As you might imagine, vegetation on the planet is markedly different during an ice age: more water becomes locked in the polar ice caps, there is less rainfall and, as a result, less plant growth. This had important implications for animals. To survive, animals adapted and adjusted to the new food chain, and humans became increasingly carnivorous.

How we have evolved metabolically

Metabolically, we are a product of this two million years of evolution and we have much in common with carnivorous animals. For example, we have a high requirement for iron, iodine and zinc, and we have only limited ability to synthesise the essential fatty acids, vitamin A and the amino acid taurine. Animal foods are the best sources of these nutrients. Our gut is significantly smaller and our brain is markedly bigger than those of other primates. This energy-demanding brain could only have come about if the gut became less demanding and the food more concentrated. This is known as the 'expensive brain hypothesis'. What does this mean for current dietary recommendations? For far too long we've assumed that humans adapt quickly and readily to radical changes in diet. In fact, our genes are still equipped for the Ice ages, not the current inter-glacial period in which agriculture made its first appearance. In other words, our genes and therefore our metabolism are programmed for nutrient intake within a well-defined range. We cannot exist on the diet of our Simian ancestors (leaves, fruit and berries). This is most clearly evident in our essential requirement for vitamin B12, which comes only from animal foods. Just as you would not expect the cat (a true carnivore) to eat grains and fruit, or the budgie to eat meat, it may be too much to expect that humans will get away with eating a diet that is too far removed from what we ate as Stone Age people.

During the past two million years of human evolution, for all but the last 10 000 years (the years since the development of agriculture), we have been hunter–gatherers rather than farmers. So what, you may ask? Well, along with farming came a big change in our diet: we started growing crops, particularly cereal grains, and, for the first time, starch entered our diet in a big way (the seeds of wild grasses being usually too small to gather

efficiently). The advent of large quantities of cereal grains tipped the ratio of animal to plant foods from being more animal to more plant. And the ratio of the major nutrients changed radically. It's a misconception that our evolutionary diet was a kind of vegetarian diet—that's true if you go back a long, long way, but it is not true of the species that evolved into Homo sapiens.

We believe it's time to look more carefully at our ancestral eating habits as a guide to the best diet for optimum health. Prehistoric hunting for meat and foraging for vegetable foods may well have provided the optimum exercise and dietary regime for human survival. The danger with the current nutritional trend towards higher carbohydrate and lower protein diets is that recommended daily intakes of animal food (meat, seafood, eggs) may be less than our bodies were designed for.

The prehistoric larder

There's little doubt that our Stone Age cousins tucked into a significantly different diet. The world's foremost authority on paleolithic diets, Dr S. Boyd Eaton of Emory University in Atlanta, has spent the past 15 years painstakingly reconstructing prehistoric diets from an array of anthropological evidence, archaeological remains and observations of surviving foraging societies. Boyd Eaton estimated

COMPARATIVE DIETS: THEN AND NOW

	PALEOLITHIC	CURRENT DIETARY GUIDELINES
Protein	20–40%	15%
Carbohydrate	20%	55%
Fat	40–60%	30%

Cordain L., Brand-Miller, J., Eaton, S. B., Mann, N., 'Plant–Animal Subsistence Ratios and Macronutrient Energy Estimations in Worldwide Hunter–Gatherer Diets', *American Journal of Clinical Nutrition*, 71 (3): 682–92, 2000.

daily paleolithic nutrient intakes from analyses of wild game animals and uncultivated vegetable foods, assuming a diet of 65 per cent plant and 35 per cent animal food (he assumed this was the average ratio based on the writing of Dr Richard Lee, author of *Man the Hunter*). Eaton's results revealed that Homo sapiens evolved on a diet low in fat, high in meat and with lower carbohydrate levels than are recommended today.

It now seems likely, however, that Boyd Eaton underestimated the amount of animal food in the average paleolithic diet. His first analysis had relied on Richard Lee's data on hunted versus gathered foods, which ignored altogether fished foods. Recently, Professor Loren Cordain, along with one of the authors of this book, published a re-analysis of the worldwide hunter–gatherer animal:plant ratios, using a much enlarged

database of hunter–gatherer groups as well as plant and animal food composition. The new analysis shows the average ratio of plant to animal foods (by energy) was 65 per cent animal food, 35 per cent plant foods. The macronutrient energy percentages generated from the re-analysis are shown in the table above.

have been efficient because of the ascorbic acid content of the non-cereal fibre. By contrast, phytic acid in the predominantly cereal-based fibre intake of industrialised nations has a well-known detrimental effect on the body's iron balance. Only small amounts of phytates in bran (5 to 10 milligrams) are needed in a meal to reduce iron absorption by half.

It is possible, however, to increase the intake of grain-based fibre without disturbing the iron balance as long as the intake of vitamin C (which is found in vegetables and fruits) is high. So early farmers who still gathered vitamin C-rich foods were protected against iron deficiency anaemia. But this is not necessarily true today: plenty of people eat too few fruits and vegetables.

Nature's fibre

Boyd Eaton believes our prehistoric relatives consumed exceedingly high levels of fibre. Fruit, roots, legumes and nuts provided the paleolithic forager with 100 grams per day of fibre compared with current recommendations of 30 grams per day. The health advantages of the high-fibre diet would have been considerable. The incidence of diabetes and colon cancer would have been extremely low. So would the problem of anaemia; by deriving fibre from fruit, nuts and vegetables, absorption of non-haem iron in the bloodstream would

Carbohydrates before agriculture

Carbohydrate levels in prehistoric diets were lower than current recommended levels (see table on page 87)—but, before the agricultural age, carbohydrates were derived almost exclusively from nuts, legumes, fruit and vegetables. So all the carbohydrate intake would have had a low glycemic index.

In addition to the well-known cancer-inhibiting effects of fruit and vegetables, the fact that our ancestors lived on more slowly digestible carbohydrates than current

PALEOLITHIC VERSUS CONTEMPORARY NUTRIENT INTAKE

VITAMINS	PALEOLITHIC	CURRENT	MINERALS	PALEOLITHIC	CURRENT
Riboflavin	6.5	1.7	Iron	87	10–15
Folate	0.36	0.18	Zinc	43	15
Thiamin	3.9	1.5	Calcium	1950	800–1200
Ascorbate	600	60	Sodium	770	500–2400
Vitamin A	17	6	Potassium	10 500	3500
Vitamin E	33	10			

The estimated daily paleolithic intake (milligrams per day) of selected nutrients compared to current recommended levels (from Boyd Eaton et al., *New England Journal of Medicine*, 1985)

agriculture-based carbohydrates (rice, corn, wheat and potatoes) is possibly significant in the etiology of diabetes and cardio-vascular disease. It may help explain why societies such as Australian Aborigines, who have skipped directly from a hunter–gatherer diet to a modern highly-digestible carbohydrate diet, suffer such high rates of diabetes and heart disease.

The mammoth eaters

The most significant difference between prehistoric and late 20th century diets is in the level of protein (see table on page 87). There is overwhelming anthropological and biochemical evidence to suggest that

paleolithic humans consumed large amounts of meat. The difference is that these days meat consumption in many countries is associated with high levels of saturated fat. The evidence from analysis of paleolithic diets suggests that game meat hunted by prehistoric humans was much lower in saturated fats than the grain-fed livestock of some Western countries.

Fortunately, Australia has the advantage of a predominantly lean meat supply. But in many countries a high animal protein diet often does go hand in hand with a high saturated fat intake and increased blood cholesterol levels. Although prehistoric hunters consumed vast amounts of cholesterol (480 mg daily, according to

Boyd Eaton), blood cholesterol levels are estimated to have been much lower than nowadays.

Boyd Eaton's analysis of paleolithic diets showed that, in contrast to the modern omega-3 to omega-6 fatty acid ratio of approximately 1:10, our prehistoric ancestors enjoyed an equivalent of 1:1 or 1:4. This had significant health benefits: a higher protein intake without raised levels of saturated fats would have improved our ancestors' blood lipid profiles. In particular, the HDL would have been higher, so the risk of chronic heart disease would probably have been lower.

The modern tendency to associate meat-eating with an increased risk of cancer and heart disease is something of a simplification. The problem arises when the meat is high in fat and when fruit and vegetable consumption is low.

Diet and survival

The evidence from paleolithic nutrition suggests that our genetic heritage was shaped over millions of years by a successful combination of animal foods, fruit and vegetables. These days, some of these foods are displaced by dairy products and grain foods, neither of which represented significant food sources in hunter-gatherer diets. Nutrient analysis of paleolithic diets explains why our ancestors had little need for today's gourmet foods and dietary supplements (see table on page 89). Their intake of essential minerals and vitamins, especially sources of vitamin C, were extraordinarily high. Even calcium intake was high, despite the lack of dairy foods. The greater satiety of high-protein foods such as meat and seafood, combined with large serves of naturally-occurring non-cereal plants, would have made for a very satisfying diet.

One diet fits all?

The current dietary recommendations are based almost entirely on dietary trials and research in Caucasians—the only population group that remains insulin sensitive in a Western environment. For most of the world's populations— including Asian, African, Asian Indian, Australian Aborigines and Pacific Islanders, who become insulin resistant if they adopt a Western lifestyle—high carbohydrate meals bring about very high blood glucose and insulin levels, which are two of the most important risk factors for mortality and morbidity. The insulin resistance and insulinemia worsen over time, especially against a backdrop of food abundance, weight gain and sedentary lifestyles.

We believe it's time to rethink our current recommended intakes in the light of the many and varied ethnic groups that make up multicultural Australia. High carbohydrate diets, especially those based on high GI foods, may not be best for everyone.

Old ways for new?

Our ancestors' diet differed vastly from our own. But the physiology and biochemistry they passed down through the generations is the same. Some nutritionists are now recommending not only a higher fruit and vegetable intake, but a higher protein and lower carbohydrate diet.

Protein is the most satiating of all the nutrients and stimulates heat production, thereby making weight control easier. Indeed, one recent study showed greater weight and fat loss on a high protein, low fat diet compared with a normal, high carbohydrate, low fat diet. High protein, low fat diets have also been shown to improve HDL and triglycerides in the blood. These findings need to be confirmed before we can recommend higher protein and lower carbohydrate diets for everyone. It is certainly not recommended for people with diabetes, in whom kidney function may be impaired.

Evolutionary considerations are not yet a basis upon which to make nutritional recommendations, but this perspective may provide valuable insights into human dietary needs and about the relationships between diet and development and diet and chronic disease.

Conventional research on nutrition sometimes produces conflicting and inconsistent findings that are hard to reconcile. An understanding of diet during human evolution can shed light on issues such as this, providing a benchmark against which the results of more traditional research can be assessed.

THE TAKE-HOME MESSAGE

- Human beings ate a high protein, low carbohydrate diet during evolution.
- On average, two-thirds of their energy came from animal foods.
- Wild animals provided varying amounts of fat (sometimes large quantities) but saturated fat intake was never high.
- A higher protein, lower carbohydrate diet may offer benefits today but people with diabetes should avoid large quantities of protein until we know more about the effects on renal disease.

A diet for today based on the diet of our ancestors

This menu derives equal proportions of energy from carbohydrate, protein and fat. We believe this may be similar in make-up to the diet eaten by humans thousands of years ago. Although the menu is based around foods we eat today, the proportions used are very different from those most people in Australia eat. For the average adult, the amount of protein is very high at 165 grams per day (the usual intake today is around 75 grams per day). In addition, all the sources of carbohydrate in this menu are slowly digested, low GI types.

Suggested quantities of each food have been included. The menu supplies 8400 kilojoules/2000 calories, with 33 per cent of energy each from carbohydrate, protein and fat. The P:M:S ratio is approximately 1:2:1.

BREAKFAST

Fruit and nut muesli with banana and yoghurt	⅓ cup rolled oats, 4 almonds, 1 tablespoon raisins, 2 teaspoons sunflower and pumpkin seeds, 1 banana and 150 g low fat plain yoghurt

MIDDAY MEAL AND SNACKS

Open roast beef sandwich with fruit	1 slice of wholegrain bread (such as Ploughman's Wholegrain™) with horseradish sauce and 60 g of lean roast beef, and a large apple
Tuna, egg and bean salad	100 g tuna, 2 hard boiled eggs, 1 tomato, 3 olives, 2 cups of lettuce and other leafy greens with 90 g mixed bean salad
Nuts and juice	50 g mixed nuts and 200 ml orange juice

EVENING MEAL

Grilled fish with lemon and steamed vegetables	200 g whole fish grilled with lemon served with 70 g butter beans and large serving of steamed broccoli, carrot, cabbage
Peaches and strawberries with honey ricotta	Diced fresh peach with 100 g strawberries served with ⅓ cup ricotta cheese and 1 tablespoon honey

putting
the life plan
into action

PART TWO

Chapter 7: **The Life Plan Way of Eating**

Chapter 8: **Get Moving!**

Chapter 9: **The Life Plan Menus**

Chapter 7

The New Glucose Revolution Life Plan Way of Eating

This section of the book is devoted to the practical details of *The New Glucose Revolution Life Plan* way of eating. In Part One we discussed five key areas of current nutrition research: the glycemic index, omega-3 fats, Mediterranean diets, Asian diets and paleolithic nutrition. We believe that aspects of the dietary regimes we have discussed in Part One hold the key to better health.

It is our aim in this section to bring together the messages contained within each of these nutritional disciplines to present you with the whole plate—a plate which incorporates low GI carbohydrate with healthy fats, lean and nutritious sources of protein and phytochemical-rich fruits and vegetables.

A nutritious diet is based on a wide variety of foods. This does not mean a wide variety of fast foods and other indulgences!

Include these foods daily:
Fresh vegetables and salad
Fresh fruit

Wholegrain bread and cereals
Low fat milk and cheese
Fish or lean meat or chicken or legumes

In addition, the following foods could be included regularly in your diet, but not necessarily daily. These foods are rich in antioxidants, vitamins and minerals. Some, such as vinegar, have a specific effect on lowering the glycemic response to carbohydrate. Others, such as nuts, olive oil and avocado, are rich in monounsaturated fats. Red wine is a traditional part of the Mediterranean diet and has been found to be cardio-protective, in moderation.

Include these foods regularly:
Nuts and seeds
Olive, canola, mustard seed oils
Avocado, olives
Dried fruit
Vinegar (vinaigrette for salads)
Red wine
Fresh herbs and spices
Shell fish and other seafoods
Omega-enriched eggs, as an alternative protein source once or twice a week

The following table illustrates how various types of protein foods and whole grains could be spread over light and main meals during the week. We encourage you to include fish one or two times a week and legumes at least twice. All meals include vegetables or salad and fruit is recommended to finish meals.

PUTTING TOGETHER MEALS FOR THE WEEK

LIGHT MEALS: wholegrain breads and cereals, low fat proteins, vegetables and salads, fruit and low fat dairy

MAIN MEALS: whole grains, low fat proteins, vegetables and salads, fruit

EXAMPLES FOR THE WEEK

	LIGHT MEALS	MAIN MEALS
MON	Felafel roll	Minestrone soup
TUES	Chicken and salad on wholegrain bread	BBQ fish with spicy couscous
WED	Chickpea curry and rice	Moroccan lamb with barley pilaf
THU	Lean beef salad and wholegrain bread	Omelette with crusty bread and salad
FRI	Pasta and seafood salad	Thai fish curry with rice
SAT	Melted cheese on wholegrain toast	Chicken and mushroom pasta
SUN	Salmon and sweetcorn patties	Roast vegetables with marinated beef

The six dietary guidelines of The Life Plan

1   EAT 7 OR MORE SERVINGS OF FRUIT AND VEGETABLES EVERY DAY

2   EAT WHOLEGRAIN BREADS AND CEREALS WITH A LOW GLYCEMIC INDEX

3   EAT MORE PULSES—BEANS, PEAS AND LENTILS—AND USE NUTS MORE FREQUENTLY

4   EAT MORE FISH AND SEAFOODS

5   EAT LEAN MEATS AND LOW FAT DAIRY FOODS

6   USE HIGH OMEGA-3 AND MONOUNSATURATED OILS SUCH AS OLIVE OIL, MUSTARD SEED OIL AND CANOLA OIL

1 EAT 7 OR MORE SERVINGS OF FRUIT AND VEGETABLES EVERY DAY

Fruit and vegetables are a major part of *The New Glucose Revolution Life Plan*. The greater the variety you eat, the better. Forget dinner plates full of plain boiled vegetables, salads of lettuce and tomato and the daily apple and banana: the variety of fruit and vegetables we are talking about extends far beyond this.

Specifically, aim at eating at least three or four different vegetables and two or three different fruits, every day. To increase your intake of ALA (the plant form of omega-3), include green vegetables, particularly green leafy vegetables. Choose from: broccoli, spinach, silverbeet, green beans, cauliflower, Brussels sprouts, leeks, cabbage, green capsicum, Asian greens.

These needn't be eaten plain. A moderate amount of a healthy oil, lemon juice, balsamic vinegar and garlic will make vegetables more appetising.

Eat a salad daily. If you or your children are not too keen on salad, serve it first and catch the appetite when it is greatest. Try a mixed salad such as coleslaw, tabbouleh or Waldorf. Make one up at the start of the weekend so you have it on hand for easy meals.

Fruit and vegetables have consistently been linked with protection from certain types of cancer. They also contain cardio-protective nutrients including unsaturated oils, fibre, vitamin B6, folate and vitamin E, which reduce our risk of heart disease. Higher consumption of vegetables, especially salad and tomatoes, decreases the risk of prostate cancer.

- Add extra vegetables (frozen are easy) to stir-fried meat.

- Chop up leftover vegetables, heat and serve as topping for toast.

- Try stuffed vegetables for something different—see our recipe for stuffed eggplant on page 185.

- Include salad ingredients in a sandwich or bread roll.

- Throw some vegies onto the BBQ with the meat. Try zucchini, corn, capsicum, mushrooms, eggplant or thick slices of par-cooked sweet potato.

- Drink vegetable juices occasionally.

- Try a vegetarian main meal dish at least once a week.

- Add grated carrot and onion to rissoles.

- Choose take-away meals that include vegetables:

  - a regular hamburger with salad
  - doner kebabs with less meat, more salad
  - Asian dishes with stir-fry veges
  - salad sandwiches or rolls
  - pasta with a Mediterranean sauce
  - vegetable pizza
  - jacket potato with beans, salsa and cheese
  - a side order of salad, not fries!

- Keep strips of celery, capsicum and carrot and florets of broccoli or cauliflower to munch on with a dip or in a lunch box for a snack.

- Try a vegetarian lasagne.

- Buy and try a vegetable that you haven't eaten before.

Tips on cooking vegetables

■ Don't overcook vegetables: cook until softened but still firm to bite.

■ To minimise the loss of vitamins and minerals from vegetables when preparing to cook them:

- Store in Long Life Vegetable Bags (available in supermarkets) in the refrigerator. These special green plastic bags slow down aging of fruit and vegetables by allowing them to breathe more easily.
- Leave the skins on where possible.
- Avoid soaking in water.
- Cook in big chunks rather than coarsely chopped.
- Never add bicarbonate of soda to the cooking water.
- Reduce the amount of water used and cover the pan.
- Cook quickly and as close to the time of serving as possible.

Tips on using more green vegetables

BUYING
Choose greens that are brightly coloured and not wilted. They taste best when very fresh so ideally shop for green vegetables two or three times a week and use within two to three days of purchase.

STORING
Loosen bunched vegetables and store loosely in a vegetable bag in the crisper. Hydroponic lettuce will keep longer if the roots are trimmed from it before storage.

PREPARING
Green leaves must be washed well to remove any fine soil or grit and then rinsed. Green leaves for a salad should be torn into small pieces rather than cut, and should be dried thoroughly before going into the salad bowl, otherwise the water will dilute the dressing. This is easily done with a 'salad spinner' or a clean tea towel.

Making the most of greens

Baby spinach salad

Baby English spinach leaves, stalks
   trimmed, washed and dried
shallots, sliced
cherry tomatoes, halved
boiled eggs, sliced

Layer these items over a large salad plate.
Top with a sprinkling of diced bacon,
cooked until crisp, and some grated
parmesan. Drizzle with vinaigrette.

Spinach in cooking

Add shredded spinach to curries, soups and
casseroles during the last couple of minutes
of cooking. Use it as part of a stuffing or
filling or layer it in a lasagne. It makes a
nutritious, easy and colourful addition. A
Mediterranean meal would usually include a
vegetable course using cauliflower, broccoli,
cabbage, spinach or silverbeet.

Stir-fried greens

Greens suitable to stir-fry include English
spinach, savoy cabbage and Chinese
greens such as bok choy, choy sum
(Chinese cabbage), gai lum (Chinese
broccoli). Separate leaves, trim stalks if
necessary, rinse under running water and
chop coarsely. Heat about 1 tablespoon of
oil (e.g. a combination of peanut and
sesame) in a wok, add the greens and stir-
fry 1 to 2 minutes. Add some freshly
minced garlic and/or ginger for flavour and
cook through until aromatic. Finish with soy
sauce or oyster sauce. Serve immediately.

Spinach with honey–soy dressing

Place washed and trimmed English spinach
leaves in a freezer bag, twisting the end to
seal. Microwave for 1 to 2 minutes.
Meanwhile, in a screw-top jar combine 1
tablespoon each of warmed honey and soy
sauce with 1 teaspoon sesame oil and
sesame seeds. Squeeze excess moisture
out of cooked spinach and toss with
dressing before serving.

Easy cooked greens

Green leafy vegetables are best cooked
with a minimum of water. You can do this
by steaming them for about 4 to 5 minutes
or cooking in a microwave with just the
water from washing clinging to the leaves
(this is easily done in a freezer bag). Finish
the cooked greens with a squeeze of
lemon, black pepper and 1 teaspoon of
canola margarine if desired.

Or, heat a teaspoon of olive oil in a large frypan. Add a clove of minced garlic and cook 1 minute. Add a bunch of trimmed and washed spinach, cover and cook a few minutes until wilted. Remove from heat and toss spinach in the juice of 1 lemon. Serve immediately.

Making the most of sweet potato

Sweet potato belongs to a different plant family to regular potato and makes an excellent low GI alternative, with a GI value of 61 compared to GI values around 80–100 for regular potatoes. The sweet flavour of sweet potato comes from naturally present sucrose (3 per cent) which increases during storage to as much as 6 per cent. Its low GI is associated with increased amounts of amylose and fibre.

It makes a great substitute for the standard pumpkin in your pumpkin soup recipe and can be added to casseroles and curries.

Roasted sweet potato

Boil or microwave peeled chunks of sweet potato until just beginning to soften on the outside. Drain and transfer to a hot baking tray brushed with oil. Brush potatoes with oil and sprinkle with seasoning (such as dried rosemary and black pepper) if desired. Bake in a hot oven (190°C) for 15 to 20 minutes until tender.

Mashed sweet potato

Mash as you would regular potato but try a little mustard seed oil in place of butter or margarine. You'll get less saturated fat, more omega-3 and a nice nutty taste.

Meatless Mediterranean roast

Toss chunks of sweet potato, lengths of zucchini, quarters of red onion and thick slices of red capsicum in olive oil seasoned with salt, pepper, dried rosemary and crushed garlic. Tip into a large baking tray and roast in a hot oven about 40 minutes. Drizzle with balsamic vinegar and serve with baked ricotta and fresh crusty bread.

Tasty wedges

Cut a large sweet potato into finger wedges. Combine a tablespoon of oil with a teaspoon of sweet paprika, a pinch of cayenne pepper or chilli powder, salt and pepper and toss the wedges in the mixture to coat. Scatter in a single layer over a large baking sheet and bake in a hot oven for about 30 minutes until tender. Spoon some low fat natural yoghurt into a dish and top with mango chutney. Serve with the wedges for dipping.

Making the most of tomatoes

The tomato plays a central role in the Mediterranean diet and is surely one of the reasons behind its benefits. Tomatoes are an almost exclusive source of the potent antioxidant lycopene, and increased consumption of tomato products has been associated with reduced risk of cancer (in particular prostate cancer) and a lower risk of heart attack. Lycopene is more bioavailable from tomato paste than fresh tomatoes, and because it is fat soluble it is more readily absorbed by the body in a meal containing some fat. So dress your tomato salad with olive oil and use a little oil when making your tomato sauce.

Basic tomato sauce

In the Mediterranean diet tomatoes are most often made into a sauce in which other vegetables are cooked. Sauté a finely chopped onion and 2 cloves of minced garlic in a tablespoon of olive oil for 3 minutes. Add an 800 gram can of crushed tomatoes, 2 tablespoons of tomato paste, 1 tablespoon of chopped basil and a teaspoon of sugar. Simmer for 15 minutes while you boil some pasta to serve it with.

Slow roasted tomatoes

Place fresh, ripe tomatoes in a bowl and cover with boiling water. Stand a couple of minutes, drain and peel off the skins. Halve the tomatoes and sit, cut side up, in a large flat baking dish or on a baking tray. Drizzle with olive oil and red wine or balsamic vinegar. Season with pepper and distribute a little crushed garlic and fresh basil over the cut halves. Bake in a moderate oven about 40 minutes. Serve at room temperature. Delicious!

Tomato salsa

Chop fresh, ripe tomatoes into small dice (removing seeds as much as possible). Combine with diced cucumber and fresh mint. Dress with olive oil and season with salt and pepper. Serve with chargrilled or pan-fried lean meat.

Making the most of fruit

You could eat more fruit by:

- Carrying a piece with you for on-the-run snacks
- Taking fruit to work every day
- Making a fruit smoothie or milkshake
- Putting a plate of sliced apple beside you to nibble on while you work, read or watch TV
- Slicing fresh fruit over your breakfast cereal
- Preparing a fruit platter for all to share after a meal
- Making sure you buy the best quality fruit you can afford and treating yourself with an exotic fruit rather than a chocolate or cake
- Keeping diced melon in a clear container in the fridge for easy consumption
- Adding sliced apple, pear, pineapple or banana to sandwich fillings or salads
- Serve slices of pan-fried apple or pear with pork

Toast thick cut slices of Tres Bon™ continental fruit loaf. Spread with light cream cheese that has been sweetened with a spoonful of caster sugar and a few drops of vanilla essence. Top with fresh fruit: sliced banana, peach, or strawberries, or whole fresh blueberries or raspberries. Dust with icing sugar to serve for a decorative touch.

Bake whole peaches or nectarines in a small amount of poaching liquid (see below) and baste with warmed honey regularly during baking (about 30 minutes). Serve with natural yoghurt.

Grill fresh whole figs by cutting a cross across the top of them and filling with finely chopped macadamia nuts and brown sugar. Place under a hot grill for 5 minutes until the sugar is melted. Serve with fresh ricotta cheese sweetened with a little honey.

Poach pears, plums, nectarines or peaches by first peeling and removing seeds. Combine 1 cup of water with ½ cup of sugar, flavour with a cinnamon stick, vanilla pod, cardamom pods or a liqueur, bring to the boil and simmer 10 minutes to create a thin syrup. Place your fruit in this and simmer 5 to 15 minutes until the fruit is tender. Serve with light vanilla fruche.

Chop up a mango, strawberries and an orange. Mix with fresh passionfruit pulp and serve with frozen yoghurt.

2 EAT WHOLEGRAIN BREADS AND CEREALS WITH A LOW GLYCEMIC INDEX

Cereal grains including rice, wheat, oats, barley, rye and products made from them (bread, pasta, breakfast cereal, flours) are the most concentrated sources of carbohydrate in our diet, with their carbohydrate contents ranging from 50 to 80 per cent of their weight. Compare this to the carbohydrate content of fruit—around 10 to 15 per cent—and root vegetables such as potato—around 15 to 20 per cent. Because of the significant amount of carbohydrate contributed by cereal grains, they have a major impact on the glycemic index of our diet.

Some might argue that the demise of the human diet began with the industrial revolution and the refining of cereal grains. Traditionally, preparation of grains was a simple process, limited to grinding between stones. So grains were retained in pretty much their original form, which meant they were slowly digested and absorbed. Our ancestors ate most of their carbohydrate in this form, including fruits, vegetables, beans and whole cereal grains—all sources of carbohydrate that have a low GI.

The advent of high-speed steel roller mills in the 19th century made the production of fine white flours and their derivatives—such as soft breads, cakes, doughnuts, corn flakes—possible. Our modern Western diet tends to be based on these quickly digested carbohydrates, which results in much greater rises in blood glucose and insulin levels than most of us have evolved to cope with. Consequently, we now suffer many diseases such as diabetes, heart disease and obesity in epidemic proportions.

So significant is the impact of the GI of our diet on our health (for more information on this see *The New Glucose Revolution*) that the WHO/FAO now recommend that preference be given to choosing foods with a low glycemic index. For these reasons we see low GI breads and cereals as a crucial part of healthy eating.

To eat breads and cereals with a low glycemic index use:

- low GI breakfast cereals (based on wheatbran, psyllium and oats)
- grainy breads made with barley, rye, linseed, triticale, sunflower seed, oats, soy and kibbled wheat
- pasta products in place of potatoes occasionally
- low GI rices with a high amylose content (such as Doongara, Basmati)

Not only do whole grains have a lower glycemic index than refined cereal grains but they are also nutritionally superior, containing higher levels of fibre, vitamins, minerals and phytoestrogens.

LOW GI BREAKFAST CEREALS

All Bran™	30
All Bran™ Fruit 'n' Oats	39
All Bran™ Soy & Fibre	33
Komplete™ Oven Baked	48
Toasted muesli	43
Natural Meusli	56
Porridge	42
Special K™	54

LOW GI BREADS

Bürgen™ Oat Bran and Honey Loaf with Barley	31
Bürgen™ Soy Lin, soy and linseed loaf	36
Bürgen™ Fruit loaf	44
Bürgen™ Mixed Grain	49
Linseed rye	55
Multi-grain™ 9-Grain	43
Performax™	38
Ploughman's Loaf™ mixed grain	47
Pumpernickel	41
Riga Sunflower and Barley	57
Sourdough rye	48
Sourdough wheat	54
Vogel's™ Honey and Oat Loaf	55

LOW GI CEREAL GRAINS

Barley	25
Buckwheat (not a true cereal)	54
Bulgur	48
Basmati rice	58
Couscous	65
Doongara rice	56

Studies show that higher consumption of whole grains is associated with reduced incidence of cancer and heart disease. A survey of 34 492 post-menopausal women (participants in the Iowa Women's Health Study) showed a clear association between whole grain intake and risk of death from ischaemic heart disease. The risk of death from ischaemic heart disease was reduced by about one-third in those women eating one or more serves of whole grain product each day.

More about cereals and grains

Barley

GI: 25

One of the oldest cultivated cereals, barley was the most important bread-making grain to the Ancient Greeks, Romans and Hebrews. It is very nutritious and high in soluble fibre, which helps to reduce the post-meal rise in blood glucose by increasing the viscosity of the intestinal contents. Look for products such as

- pearl barley and Barley Quick™ to use in soups, stews, pilafs
- barley flakes or rolled barley, which have a light, nutty flavour and can be cooked as a porridge and used in baked goods and stuffings

Bulgur

GI: 48

Bulgur is an ancient wheat product that is still widely used in Eastern Europe. It is made from wheat grains that have been hulled and steamed before grinding to crack the grain. It is also known as cracked wheat. The particular value of bulgur lies in the fact that the whole wheat grain remains virtually intact—it is simply cracked—and the wheat germ and bran are retained. This retains nutrients and lowers the GI Bulgur is used as the base of the Middle Eastern salad tabbouleh, but can also be cooked quickly (boil in an equal volume of water for 15 minutes) and used as a base for pilafs, burgers or stuffings.

Corn/maize

GI of sweetcorn: 46

Corn was first used on a domestic scale 10 000 years ago in South America and became the staple of the whole of the American subcontinent. To this day, corn underpins the American economy not only as a food for humans and animals but also as a component of many products (paper and packaging, soaps, insecticides, cosmetics, detergents and adhesives are just some products which contain corn). Sweetcorn is an excellent source of fibre and a popular vegetable with children. Fresh, frozen and canned varieties of sweetcorn have a low GI. Even popcorn has a low GI and is healthiest prepared at home from bagged popping corn in an air popper. Products like corn chips and cornflakes do not share the low GI of corn.

Oats

GI of porridge: 42

Wholegrain oats that have been hulled, steamed and flattened are known to us as rolled oats. This popular cereal grain is useful in lowering the GI of the diet as porridge, muesli, or in biscuits, bread and meatloaves. Oat bran also has a low GI.

Here is a simple recipe for a low GI oat biscuit, made without any flour:

OAT BISCUITS

Melt 50 grams of canola margarine in a frying pan. Add 200 grams of rolled oats. Stir over heat to brown the oats lightly. Cool. Beat one egg with 100 g of sugar until foamy. Add some vanilla essence or lemon zest and 3 to 4 tablespoons of milk. Stir in the cooled oats and 1 level teaspoon of baking powder. Form into walnut-sized balls and place on a baking tray lined with a sheet of baking paper. Cook for 15 minutes in a hot oven.

Rice

GI factor varies: see table on page 80

Rice can have a high GI (80–90) or a low GI (50–55) depending on the variety and, in particular, its amylose content. Amylose is a type of starch that is more slowly digested and gives foods a lower GI. Most Australian rices are about 20 per cent amylose and 80 per cent amylopectin. Amylopectin has a branched structure, making it more accessible to digestive enzymes and more readily digested to glucose. High amylopectin starch produces a higher glycemic response. Doongara (GI 56) and Basmati rice (GI 58) contain higher proportions of amylose which is more compact in structure, more slowly digested and produces a lower glycemic response. Waxy or glutinous rice, which becomes sticky when cooked, has a high GI. It is preferred for rice desserts, particularly in Asia. Arborio rice, which is especially good for making risotto, releases its starch during cooking and is likely to have a high GI because of this. Japonica rice is a short grain variety, eaten all over Japan, which has a low GI. This may not translate into sushi being low GI since the rice used in making sushi is coated with corn syrup and cornstarch, both high GI forms of carbohydrate.

Rye

Whole kernel rye has a GI of 34

Rye as a crop was first planted by the Romans and by the Middle Ages had become a staple throughout Europe. In Eastern Europe, especially Germany, rye has retained its popularity, and Russians and Scandinavians prefer the flavour of dark rye bread. Whole kernel rye is used to make breads, pumpernickel bread and some crispbreads. Rye flakes are similar to rolled oats and may be eaten as porridge or sprinkled over bread before baking.

Wheat

GI of whole wheat kernels: 41

Wheat is a universal grain, providing a staple food to half the world's population. Whole wheat needs to be soaked overnight and can then be simmered for about 1 hour to use as a base for pilaf or as a porridge. Sprouted grains of whole wheat make a delicious addition to salads.

Quick ideas with pasta and noodles

Vegetable and noodle stir-fry

Fresh noodles from refrigerated section
   of supermarket
Baby corn
Snow peas, baby spinach, choy sum
   or other leafy green
Red capsicum
Shallots
Garlic and ginger
Teriyaki or oyster sauce
Sesame oil

Place the noodles in a bowl and cover with boiling water. Chop and stir-fry vegetables in sesame oil, starting with the firmer pieces. Drain the noodles, add to wok with vegetables and drizzle with sauce to taste.

Instant noodles

Packets of instant noodles have become a popular snack these days but most brands contain significant amounts of fat and salt. Next time you buy them look for the packets of plain noodle cakes with no added fats or oils. Add your own flavouring using Massel salt-reduced stock powder and a handful of mixed fresh or frozen vegetables.

Mediterranean pasta sauce

Onion
Capsicum
Canned tomatoes
Marinated artichoke hearts (available in jars
   at the supermarket and from
   delicatessens)
Black olives
Garlic

Sauté a large chopped onion. Add some diced capsicum, canned chopped tomatoes, artichoke hearts, black olives and minced garlic. Bring to the boil then simmer 10 to 15 minutes (uncovered to reduce if needed). Serve over pasta.

Seared Atlantic Salmon Fillets with White Bean Puree, page 202

EAT MORE PULSES—BEANS, PEAS AND LENTILS—AND USE NUTS MORE FREQUENTLY

Pulses, including lentils, chickpeas, soybeans and kidney beans, are an important part of a low GI diet. It is recommended that you eat them at least twice a week. The average Australian's intake of these foods is low, being less than 5 grams a day versus the 30 or more grams per day eaten by Asian and Mediterranean populations. Easy ways to eat pulses include using them in soups, salads and sauces.

Pulses are nutrient dense, providing protein, iron, zinc, calcium, folate and soluble fibre. They are also an excellent source of phytoestrogens such as lignans and isoflavones. Epidemiological studies suggest that large consumption of phytoestrogens confers a reduced risk of several diseases. The oestrogenic and antioestrogenic activity of lignans and isoflavones, for example, has proved useful in controlling the symptoms of menopause. Lignans and isoflavones possess antiviral, antifungal, antibacteriocidal and anticarcinogenic properties. Flavones also have antihypertensive, anti-inflammatory and antioxidant activities. Beans are high in folate, which lowers the level of homocysteine in the blood and reduces the risk of cardiovascular disease.

Pulses are:

- low cost
- low in kilojoules
- free of saturated fat and cholesterol
- filling

Soybeans are particularly rich in ALA (the plant precursor of omega-3) compared to other pulses, and also contain genistein—an anti-cancer phytochemical. Tofu (soy bean curd) is an easy way of using soy. It has a mild flavour itself but absorbs the flavours of other foods so is delicious marinated in soy sauce, ginger and garlic and tossed into a stir-fry. Try our recipe for Tofu Chicken with Snow Peas and Hokkien Noodles on page 182.

Pulses supply carbohydrate, protein but very little fat. They are high in fibre—both soluble and insoluble—and are a great source of vitamins. Although they will keep indefinitely, dried pulses are best used within one year of purchase. Young beans cook faster than old ones and will also have stronger colours.

Cornmeal, Capsicum and Chive Muffins, page 158

1. **Soak**. Place in a saucepan and cover with 2 to 3 times their volume of cold water. Soak overnight or during the day.
   Shortcut: Rather than soaking overnight, add 3 times the volume of water to rinsed beans, bring to the boil for a few minutes then remove from heat and let soak for an hour. Drain, add fresh water and cook as usual.

2. **Cook**. Drain off soaking water, adding 2 to 3 times the volume of water as beans. Bring to the boil then simmer until tender. Use directions on the packet or the information below as a guide to time.

   - Don't add salt to the cooking water of pulses—it slows down water absorption so cooking takes longer.

   - Don't cook beans in the water they have soaked in. Substances that contribute to flatulence are leached from the beans into the soaking and cooking waters.
     Shortcuts: Precooked canned and vacuum-packed pulses are the shortcut to cooking with beans. Meals made with these can be prepared in less time than meat meals. Quickpulse™ is an Australian company that produces precooked pulses in vacuum-sealed plastic packs. They are cooked and packaged at low temperatures to retain more nutrients. They require no refrigeration and are available through health food stores and some supermarkets.

   - Precook your own dried pulses and freeze in small batches.

   - Soaked or cooked beans can be kept several days in the fridge.

   - One 440 g can of beans substitutes for 3/4 cup of dried beans.

Some varieties of beans

Chickpeas (also known as garbanzo beans)

These large, caramel-coloured legumes are popular in Middle Eastern and Mediterranean dishes. Buy in cans or pre-cooked in a vacuum pack. To cook your own, cover a bowl of dried chickpeas with plenty of cold water and soak overnight. Drain, put in saucepan and cover with clean water. Bring to the boil, boil for 10 minutes then simmer 1.5 hours until tender to bite.

Red kidney beans

These are the red beans you find in Mexican dishes such as chilli con carne, nachos and tacos. They are very easily added to mincemeat dishes to make them go further and add nourishment: just open a can and drain them. Dried beans should be soaked overnight. Drain, rinse, adding fresh water, and boil 15 minutes then simmer 1 to 1.5 hours.

Split peas

Green or yellow split peas are great to add to soups and will cook in about 40 minutes without pre-soaking. Green split peas are traditionally used in pea and ham soup and both are a component of dried soup mix.

Lentils

Lentils are available as either whole green or brown, whole red or split red. The split lentils are relatively quick to cook, needing to simmer, partly covered for only 10 to 15 minutes, without pre-soaking. Whole brown lentils are available now in cans and in vacuum packs. The dried whole lentils will need to be boiled for about 45 minutes.

Cannellini beans

These are small white beans available dried or in cans (often sold as butter beans). They have a nice mild flavour. Dried beans need to be soaked overnight. Drain, then rinse and add fresh water. Boil for 15 minutes and then simmer for 1 to 1.5 hours to make them tender.

Using chickpeas

For all these ideas you need cooked chickpeas. The quickest way to get these is from the supermarket in a vacuum pack (Quickpulse™) or from a can. Alternatively, you can soak and cook your own (see intructions on previous page) and freeze them in 1 or 2 cup batches ready to defrost when needed.

Chickpea burgers

Cooked and drained chickpeas
Mashed potato
Egg
Shallots
Mint
Cumin
Lemon juice

Place approximately 2 cups of drained chickpeas in the bowl of a food processor and process until coarsely chopped. Add an equal volume (about 2 cups) of mashed potato, a handful of chopped shallots, juice of a lemon, clove of crushed garlic, teaspoon of cumin and 1 egg. Process to combine. Shape into patties and pan fry until golden (about 5 minutes each side). Serve onto plates and top with a dollop of low fat natural yoghurt and mango chutney. Accompany with mixed salad leaves.

Chickpea curry

Cooked and drained chickpeas
Onion
Minced garlic and ginger
Curry paste or powder
Canned tomatoes
Potato
Pumpkin
Green beans

Heat 2 teaspoons of oil in a large frypan, adding a teaspoon of minced ginger, garlic and 1 diced onion. When softened, add a

dessertspoonful of your favourite curry paste or curry powder. Cook a few minutes then add a can of chopped tomatoes, 1 ½ cups chickpeas, 1 diced potato and some diced pumpkin, cover and simmer for 20 minutes. Add a handful of halved green beans and cook 5 minutes more. Serve with Basmati rice.

Hummus (chickpea dip)

Purchase in the refrigerator section of the supermarket or make your own using the recipe on page 161. Hummus is delicious spread on toasted Turkish bread and eaten with olives or tabbouli.

Warm chickpea salad

Cooked and drained chickpeas
Tomatoes
Red (Spanish) onion
Parsley
Vinaigrette

Place 4 ripe tomatoes in a bowl. Cover with boiling water, leave 1 minute and then peel off their skins. Halve the tomatoes and place on a lined baking tray. Top each half with a spot of olive oil, some black pepper and a little crushed garlic. Chop a red onion into quarters and place amongst the tomatoes. Roast at 200°C for about 40 minutes and then allow to cool slightly. To serve, divide the tomatoes and onion between 4 serving plates. Distribute a

400 g can of drained chickpeas over the top. Drizzle with a garlic vinaigrette and finish with a sprinkling of chopped parsley.

Chick nuts

Toss 2 cups of cooked and drained chickpeas in a spice mixture made up of ½ teaspoon each of cumin, chilli powder, paprika, ground coriander and salt and 2 teaspoons of castor sugar. Heat 1 tablespoon of peanut or canola oil in a large frypan, add the chickpeas and cook, stirring often for about 5 minutes until browned. Transfer the chickpeas onto paper towel or a wire rack to cool and store in an airtight container. They will keep for about a week.

Making the most of nuts

In a Mediterranean diet, nuts and seeds (including almonds, walnuts, pumpkin and sunflower seeds, tahini and roasted chickpeas) are eaten once or twice a week. Research suggests that a small handful of nuts (30 g) on most days of the week is beneficial in lowering cholesterol and reducing risk of heart attack. Nuts contain:
- very little saturated fat (they are predominantly mono- or polyunsaturated)
- dietary fibre
- vitamin E, an antioxidant believed to be important in preventing heart disease

Walnuts and pecans also contain some omega-3 fats. Linseeds are very rich in omega-3, providing as much as 11 grams of plant omega-3 per tablespoon. They are also rich in lignan and plant oestrogens. When freshly ground, linseeds have a subtle nutty flavour and can be added to breads, muffins, biscuits and cereals.

Easy ways to eat more nuts

- Use nuts and seeds in food preparation: for example, toasted cashews or sesame seeds in a chicken stir-fry, walnuts sprinkled over a salad, toasted almonds over a fruity dessert
- Spread bread with peanut butter or tahini rather than butter or margarine
- Sprinkle a mixture of ground nuts and linseeds over cereal or salads, or add to baked goods like muffins
- Enjoy nuts as a snack. Although high in fat, nuts make a healthy substitute for less nutritious high fat snacks such as potato crisps, chocolate and biscuits

EAT MORE FISH AND SEAFOODS

Regular fish consumption is consistently associated with reduced risk of coronary heart disease. In fact, one serving of fish weekly has been found to reduce our risk of a fatal heart attack by 40 per cent. The likely protective components of fish are the very long chain omega-3 fatty acids: eicosapentanoic acid (EPA) and docosahexanoic acid (DHA). Our bodies only make small amounts of these fatty acids and so we rely on dietary sources. (See Chapter 3 for more on the benefits of omega-3 fats.)

While the very long chain omega-3 fats are also found in some other animal foods, Australian seafood contains 10 to 100 times more than is found in other food groups. For this reason we suggest that you aim to include at least one fish meal per week. This amount appears to be sufficient to reduce coronary heart disease risk, and we do not yet know if more frequent intake confers other benefits. In a traditional Mediterranean diet, fish and seafood would usually be included once or twice a week. The Heart Foundation recommends that adult Australians should aim to include at least 2 fish meals per week in their diet.

It is important that your fish meals do not contain excessive amounts of saturated fat through frying in solid fat. That means fried fish from the fish shop

doesn't count, nor do pre-cooked crumbed frozen fish products that have been cooked in saturated oils.

Which fish is best?

Oily fish, which tend to have darker coloured flesh and a stronger fishy flavour, are the richest source of omega-3 fats. (Don't be put off by the term fatty or oily fish: 100 grams of the fattiest fish has about the same amount of fat as 200 grams of very lean beef.)

Canned salmon, sardines, mackerel and, to a lesser extent, tuna are very rich sources. Canned fish should be purchased as canned in brine, water or springwater.

Fresh fish with higher levels of omega-3 are: Atlantic salmon and smoked salmon, blue and Spanish mackerel, gemfish, sea mullet, tailor and Southern blue fin tuna. Sydney rock oysters, arrow squid and southern calamari are also a rich source.

'But I don't like seafood!'

If you don't like fish or seafood you will obtain some omega-3 fatty acids from lean red meat and omega-enriched eggs. You can also obtain a precursor of these very long chain fatty acids from plants. This precursor is also an omega-3 fat known as alpha-linolenic acid (ALA). Our body can convert this plant-based omega-3 fat to EPA and DHA but it takes about 10 grams

of ALA to yield 1 gram of DHA and EPA. ALA is found in linseed, canola, walnut and soybean oils. There are also small amounts in walnuts, linseeds, pecans, soybeans, baked beans, wheatgerm, lean meats, and green leafy vegetables.

Fish oil supplements are another alternative, but you are unlikely to get the full benefit of increased omega-3 intake without modifying your diet in other ways as well. Choose a capsule with the largest amount of EPA + DHA. Take care—in a 1000 milligram capsule the amount of EPA + DHA can vary considerably. Vitamin E should also be included in the capsule to help prevent the fish oils from oxidising.

Is cod liver oil a source of omega-3 fatty acids?

Although cod liver oil contains some long chain omega-3 fats, the amounts are quite small. What it does contain a lot of is vitamins A and D, two fat soluble vitamins that are stored in our body. Taking enough cod liver oil to meet our omega-3 requirement would exceed the recommended intake of these vitamins.

Ways with canned fish

Salmon and butter bean salad

Canned salmon
Lebanese cucumber
Red (Spanish) onion
Canned butter beans

Drain a small can of salmon and break into chunks. Drain a small can of butter beans. Combine beans and salmon with 1 diced cucumber and 1/2 red onion in a bowl. In a screw-top jar combine 1 tablespoon each of olive oil and lemon juice. Add a clove of crushed garlic and black pepper. Pour over salad. Pack in a sealed container and team with low GI bread for lunch.

Sardine toast topper

Sardines canned in springwater
Garlic
Capers
Pitted black olives
Parsley
White vinegar
Olive oil

Drain a can of sardines and place in a food processor with a clove of crushed garlic, a tablespoon of drained capers, about eight pitted black olives, 1/2 bunch of chopped parsley, a tablespoon of vinegar and a tablespoon of olive oil. Process until just combined and spread on a low GI bread, toasted.

Lunchtime tuna

Sandwich tuna in brine or water
Celery, shallots or salad onion
Canola mayonnaise

Add diced celery and onion to drained tuna.
Mix with a dollop of mayonnaise and
season with black pepper. Use as a
sandwich filling without any butter or
margarine.

Tuna with vegie toss

To leftover or fresh boiled small pasta (for
example, bows or spirals) add a can of
drained tuna (or salmon), crushed garlic,
black pepper, chopped fresh herbs such as
parsley and basil, and a drizzle of olive oil.
Mix in some reheated leftover vegetables
such as zucchini, mushroom, broccoli or
capsicum.

Ways with fish fillets

Fish is quick and easy to cook. Cutlets of
fish such as swordfish, salmon, blue eye
cod or Spanish mackerel take 2½ to 3
minutes each side or 5 to 6 minutes total:

- in a non-stick pan over medium heat,
  with a film of oil or cooking spray
- under a pre-heated grill
- on a BBQ hotplate or chargrill, brushed
  with flavoured oil
- steamed or poached with a little white
  wine or lemon juice

- baked for 10 to 15 minutes in a
  moderate oven.

Good grilled fish fillets

Try fillets of bream or ocean perch, flake
or ling. Preheat grill on high. Line a baking
tray with foil and place fish skin side down.
Brush fish with a little olive oil and sprinkle
with black pepper. Cook under hot grill
3 to 4 minutes, turning halfway through
cooking. To test if it's ready, the fish should
flake with a fork. It is best served with
fresh lemon.

Fish with tomato and beans

White fish fillets such as hoki or ling
Tomatoes
Red or white onion
Green beans

Quickly cook the beans in the microwave
until just tender–crisp.
Refresh under cold water. Combine in a
bowl with sliced tomatoes, thinly sliced
onion, chopped parsley, and a tablespoon
each of olive oil and lemon juice. Mix, then
serve onto plates. Brush fish fillets with a
little olive oil, season with pepper and cook
on a preheated grill or BBQ for 2 to 3
minutes each side. Serve on top of
the salad.

5 EAT LEAN MEATS AND LOW FAT DAIRY FOODS

Eating lean meats and low fat dairy foods takes you a good step towards eating a diet that is low in saturated fat. Scientists have known for years that a diet high in saturated fats raises cholesterol levels and increases heart disease risk, and more recently saturated fats, specifically, have been implicated in contributing to insulin resistance and obesity. Saturated fat (compared to other fats) is poorly oxidised (burned) to yield energy and therefore appears to be more readily stored. In contrast, omega-3 polyunsaturated and monounsaturated fatty acids are more likely to be used for energy rather than storage.

Saturated fats should comprise less than 10 per cent of our total kilojoule intake. For an average adult eating around 7500 to 8500 kilojoules, this equates to about 20 grams of saturated fat per day. Unfortunately, the message to 'avoid saturated fat' has, for many people, translated into 'avoid red meat and dairy products'—removing primary sources of iron and calcium from their diet. While it is true that these two food groups could contribute saturated fat to our diet, avoiding these foods entirely will not result in a healthy diet.

We suggest eating lean meat 2 or 3 times a week, accompanied by salad and vegetables. Trim all visible fat from meat,

especially pork, and remove the skin (and fat just below it) from chicken. Game meat such as kangaroo, rabbit and venison are not only lean meats but are good sources of omega-3 fatty acids, as are organ meats such as liver and kidney. Replacing full fat dairy foods with reduced fat or low fat varieties will also considerably reduce saturated fat intake.

Much of the saturated fat we are consuming these days comes from pre-prepared packaged and take-away foods. Tallow and palm oil are the most commonly used commercial frying fats but both are highly saturated. Until greater efforts are made by commercial providers of food to reduce the saturated fat content of their product, it is appropriate to eat only the occasional fried fast food.

The place for cholesterol-rich foods such as eggs

It used to be thought that eating foods high in cholesterol such as eggs, offal, prawns and other crustaceans would raise our blood cholesterol levels. This has been found to be incorrect, because our body compensates for the increased cholesterol intake by reducing cholesterol production by the liver (although a small percentage of people have an inherited condition that impairs this self-regulation). This means that you could eat an egg a day, for example, without any harm to heart health. To enhance your intake of omega-3 fats we suggest using omega-3 enriched eggs which have around six times more ALA and DHA than regular eggs. They are produced by feeding hens a diet that is naturally rich in omega-3 (including canola and linseeds).

Ways with lean meat

BBQ

Beef: Use New York cut steak (boneless sirloin), scotch fillet (rib eye), rump fillet, oyster blade, eye of silverside
Lamb: Trim lamb steaks, lamb backstrap or eye of loin and lamb fillet are all ideal to barbecue or chargrill.

Simply brush with oil (adding flavourings such as garlic or herbs if you like) to stop sticking and drying out. Preheat the BBQ or grill and cook 3 to 4 minutes each side for medium rare or 4 to 5 minutes each side for well done. Rest a couple of minutes after cooking then slice across the grain. Toss with:

- salad greens and balsamic dressing
- chopped tomato, cucumber and mint combined with olive oil, salt and pepper

Warm lamb salad

Pan fry trim lamb steaks (allowing one per person) in a little olive oil or cooking spray for about 3 minutes each side. Remove and set aside to rest. Add 1 tablespoon oil and 1 tablespoon balsamic vinegar to the pan, stir to combine and remove from heat. Slice the lamb steaks and combine with canned tiny new potatoes, quartered; cherry tomatoes, halved; red capsicum, cut into thin strips; and baby spinach leaves. Pour warm dressing over salad and toss through. Serve immediately.

Chilli beef

Take 500 grams of lean beef strips and mix with 2 teaspoons of canola oil and a teaspoon of minced garlic. Stir-fry in batches and set aside. Stir-fry whatever vegetables you have on hand (such as fine cut sections of onion, finely sliced carrot, capsicum, zucchini, snow peas) and return beef to the pan. Stir in 2 teaspoons each of red curry paste and sweet chilli sauce with some fresh basil and cherry tomato halves. Heat through and serve with rice or noodles.

Mediterranean casserole

Begin casserole in the usual way, sautéing a chopped onion and browning some lean cubed beef or lamb. Add canned tomatoes with juice then diced red capsicum, button mushrooms, fresh herbs such as oregano and basil, black olives and some red wine. Cover and simmer or bake slowly, until the meat is tender—about 1½ to 2 hours. If the casserole is too thin, simmer uncovered on the stove to reduce the liquid.

FOODS HIGH IN SATURATED FATS

FOOD TYPE	SATURATED FAT CONTENT (G)
Potato crisps (50 g bag)	7
Corn chips (50 g bag)	6
Croissant	6
Meat pie	13
Sausage roll	15
Fried chicken (1 piece)	7
Doughnut	5
Medium thickshake	7
Medium French fries	11
Chump chop with fat	5
Sausages (1)	5
Whole milk (1 cup)	6
Whipped cream (2 tablespoons)	5
Cheese (2 bread-size slices from block)	6
Chicken nuggets (6)	8
Ice-cream (2 scoops)	6
Hot chips (1 cup)	10
Sweet and sour pork with fried rice	16
Pizza with meat and cheese toppings (2 slices)	12
Butter (1 tablespoon)	10
Dripping or lard (1 tablespoon)	10
Coconut milk and cream (½ cup)	26

 USE HIGH OMEGA-3 AND MONOUNSATURATED OILS SUCH AS OLIVE OIL, MUSTARD SEED OIL AND CANOLA OIL

The following oils are rich in monounsaturated fatty acids, which should supply the majority of fat in our diet.

Olive oil has been a part of the Mediterranean and Middle Eastern diet for thousands of years. It is recognised as a healthy alternative to other fats and oils because it is high in monounsaturated fats and low in saturates. Its minimal content of polyunsaturated fatty acids is also an advantage because it allows our body to make greater use of the polyunsaturated omega-3 fats we obtain from other dietary sources, without any competition from excessive polyunsaturated omega-6 fats. (See pages 40 and 41 for more details.)

Olive oil has other virtues, being rich in antioxidants and a substance called squalene that has anti-inflammatory properties, slows blood clot formation and lowers cholesterol.

Canola and mustard seed oil, besides being high in monounsaturated fat, contain significant amounts of ALA, the plant form of polyunsaturated omega-3 fat. Canola oil contains approximately 2 grams of ALA per tablespoon and mustard seed oil about 3 grams per tablespoon. Mustard seed oil has the lowest saturated fat content of any

TYPES OF FAT AND THEIR SOURCES

There is less evidence to support a further reduction in the amount of fat we eat than there is to recommend for changing the type. Although foods contain a mixture of fatty acids, one type of fatty acid tends to predominate, allowing us to categorise foods according to their main fatty acid component.

An asterisk next to a food in the following list indicates a good source of omega-3 fatty acids.

POLYUNSATURATED PRODUCTS

OILS
Safflower, sunflower, grapeseed, soybean*, corn, linseed* (flaxseed), cottonseed, walnut*, sesame, evening primrose oils

SPREADS
Polyunsaturated margarines, tahini (sesame seed paste)

NUTS AND SEEDS
Walnuts, sunflower seeds, pumpkin seeds (pepitas), sesame seeds

OTHER PLANT SOURCES
Soybeans, soy milk, wheatgerm, whole grains

Animal sources
Oily fish*

MONOUNSATURATED PRODUCTS

OILS
Olive, canola*, peanut, Sunola™, macadamia and mustard seed oils

SPREADS
Monounsaturated margarines made from these oils*, peanut butter

NUTS AND SEEDS
Cashews, macadamias, almonds, hazelnuts, pecans, pistachio, peanuts

OTHER PLANT SOURCES
Avocado, olives

ANIMAL SOURCES
Very lean red meat, lean chicken, lean pork, egg yolk, omega-enriched eggs*

SATURATED PRODUCTS

OILS/FATS
Palm and palm kernel oil, coconut oil, dripping, lard, copha, ghee, solid frying oils and cooking margarines

SPREADS
Butter, cream cheese

DAIRY FOODS
Full cream dairy products: cheese, cream, sour cream, yoghurt, whole milk, ice-cream

ANIMAL SOURCES
Fat on beef, lamb, skin on chicken, sausage, salami, luncheon meats

Australian oil. It is produced through cold pressing which is likely to retain more antioxidants. (see Cold pressed oils below).

Margarines are available based on canola and olive oils. Olive oil based spreads contain almost equal parts of olive and canola oils. We suggest you spread it thinly.

Linseed oil is the richest plant source of ALA (one tablespoon provides approximately 9 grams) and it contains very little omega-6 fat. But linseed oil is highly prone to oxidation—meaning the fats it contains turns rancid easily. For this reason, we suggest using linseeds as a source of ALA rather than linseed oil.

Sunola oil is another highly monounsaturated oil. It is a genetic variant of sunflower oil and is very heat stable so makes an ideal alternative to the saturated fats that are normally used commercially for frying. It contains little or no ALA or LA and so, like olive oil, is omega neutral.

Cold pressed oils are among those that have undergone minimal processing. Recent research suggests that these oils may be better for our heart because they are richer in compounds called polyphenols, which have antioxidant properties. In 'cold pressed' oils, the oil is extracted from the seed, nut or fruit by mechanical pressing only, without the use of heat or solvents. Oils obtained by this method have a stronger flavour and colour than their regular counterparts. They are also much richer in vitamin E (a natural preservative present in oils) and other antioxidants. For example, extra-virgin olive oil—the best quality oil made from the first cold pressing of the olives—contains 30 to 40 different antioxidants. Mustard seed oil is a naturally mild flavoured and coloured cold pressed oil.

Light and extra light oils are those oils that are light in colour and flavour. The terms 'light' and 'extra light' don't mean the oil is lower in fat than any other oil.

Ways with olive oil

When storing olive oil, keep the air space in the bottle to a minimum to reduce oxidation (rancidity) and store in a cool, dark place (but don't refrigerate). Buy only small bottles of oil, or if buying larger amounts, consider decanting into smaller airtight bottles. And remember, unlike wine, olive oil does not improve with age!

Marinade

A delicious marinade for lamb can be made by combining 1/4 cup of white wine with 1 tablespoon each of lemon juice, olive oil and honey, with minced garlic and fresh or dried rosemary.

Croutons

A scattering of tasty toasted croutons makes a green salad all the more enjoyable. Traditionally made with butter, they are delicious made with olive oil.

2 slices Bürgen™ grain bread, cut into
    small cubes
Olive oil
Finely grated parmesan cheese
Crushed garlic

Toss the cubes of bread in a bowl with 1 tablespoon of olive oil, a tablespoon of parmesan cheese and a clove of crushed garlic. Spread out onto a baking sheet and bake in a preheated hot oven for 10 minutes. Remove and cool before using.

Tomato and olive vinaigrette

In a screw-top jar combine 4 tablespoons olive oil with the juice of 1 lemon, 1 tablespoon of white wine vinegar, a clove of crushed garlic and a teaspoon of grainy mustard. Add 1 tablespoon of finely chopped continental parsley, 1 small tomato that has been very finely diced and 3 to 4 finely diced pitted black olives. Shake to combine. Stand about 30 minutes before serving.

Mediterranean-style dressing

In a screw-top jar, combine 2 tablespoons of olive oil and with 1 tablespoon of red wine or balsamic vinegar. Add 1 clove of crushed garlic, black pepper, salt and fresh herbs to your liking.

Vinegar

Recent reports in the scientific literature have shown that vinegar or lemon juice consumed with a meal has significant blood glucose lowering effects. As little as 1 tablespoon of vinegar in a vinaigrette dressing, taken with an average meal, lowered blood glucose by as much as 30 per cent. The effect appears to be related to the acidity, which may work by slowing stomach emptying and thereby slowing carbohydrate digestion. Studies at the University of Sydney measured the greatest effect with red wine vinegar and lemon juice, but we have used a range of vinegars in the recipes throughout this book.

Balsamic vinegar: a rich, dark vinegar made from sweet wine aged in wooden barrels. It has a sweet, sharp flavour.

Wine vinegar: made from red or white grapes and popular for salad dressings. It is often flavoured with herbs such as tarragon.

Rice wine vinegar: a mild flavoured vinegar distilled from fermented rice.

Deep Sea Perch on Roasted Vegetables, page 198

THE TAKE-HOME MESSAGE

■ Eat 'good' fats, and foods that contain these fats, more freely—don't go overboard!

■ We still need to limit fatty meats and full cream dairy foods.

■ Limit commercially prepared foods that contain palm and coconut oils and hydrogenated fat.

■ Include: oils, such as olive and canola; lean meats, especially game meat; fish and seafoods, including oily fish. Include nuts, seeds and omega-enriched eggs in moderate amounts.

Chapter 8

Get Moving!

Did you notice we used the word 'moving' not 'exercising'? There's a good reason. Most people think of exercise as a formal, structured and timed event in their lives. While some people can and do make a serious commitment to 20 to 30 minutes of exercise 3 to 4 times a week, the majority of us say we are too busy and don't have the time. The result—no attempt at all. We are disinclined to make any effort or commitment: too tired, too rushed, too stressed, too hot, too cold— the list of excuses goes on. But there's good news: we don't need exercise, we just need movement.

In the beginning, the experts told us that unless our exercise was vigorous and sustained for 20 to 30 minutes, we needn't bother. However, we now realise this was incorrect advice. It appears that any amount of movement is better than none at all. Can you accumulate 30 minutes of moving around each day? Say, 5 minutes of weeding here, 10 minutes walking to the shops and back, 2 minutes walking up and down the stairs, etc. This is all it takes to obtain measurable health benefits.

It doesn't need to vigorous to be beneficial. You just need to get moving! And it doesn't need to involve gyms, special equipment or expensive venues and accessories.

Walking fits the bill perfectly. Humans were purpose built to walk upright—it's the most natural, the safest and the easiest form of physical activity there is.

Walking for pleasure and health

Walking is so good for you! And it becomes even more important as we grow older. Walking at a comfortable speed has proven benefits on heart and lung function. It is good for general fitness as well as being safe, cheap and convenient. It can be enjoyed alone or with friends. Talking while you walk can have important mental benefits: not only do we produce calming hormones while we walk, but the talk itself can be great therapy—good for relationships in general. So instead of saying 'Would you like a cup of tea?' say 'Would you like to take a stroll?' But don't hesitate to walk alone if you prefer, or walk the dog—your pet will love you all the more for it. You'll find yourself with time to think and relax.

The following tips have been taken (with permission) from Active Australia's 'Walking for Pleasure and Health' booklet, a recent government initiative to promote a form of exercise that is available to everybody, regardless of age and fitness.

Walking regularly has scientifically proven benefits. You will tend to (no kidding!):

- feel more confident, happy and relaxed
- control your weight better
- improve your blood cholesterol levels
- have lower blood pressure
- have stronger bones (less chance of osteoporosis)
- be less likely to have a heart attack
- recover better from heart attack
- be less likely to have a stroke
- be less likely to develop diabetes in middle age

HOW OFTEN?

Try to walk every day. Ideally we should accumulate 30 minutes or more on most days of the week. You can do it in two 15 minute stints or six 5-minute stints. It doesn't matter.

HOW HARD?

You should be able to talk comfortably while you walk. Find a level that suits YOU.

Getting started

Before getting started, see your doctor if you:

- have not been active for some time
- have a history of heart disease or chest pains
- have diabetes
- are very overweight
- are a smoker
- have high blood pressure

Sore feet show on your face

The most important walking equipment is a pair of sturdy, comfortable, lightweight walking shoes. If your feet feel good, you will walk well and continue to want to. It's worth the investment. Some health funds will cover part of the cost of walking shoes.

STOP PRESS!

A new study has revealed that greater physical activity is associated with a lower risk of developing type 2 diabetes. The exercise did not need to be intense—exercise of moderate duration and intensity, **including walking**, was associated with reduced risk of disease. While brisk walking was best, even the slow walkers benefited!

1   Wear a broad-brimmed hat and sunglasses and use a sunscreen on exposed skin. Don't forget the top of the feet if exposed. Avoid the hours between 10 a.m. and 2 p.m. (11 a.m. and 3 p.m. during daylight saving). Keep to the shady side of the street.

2   Wear well-cushioned flat-soled shoes and layers of clothing that can be removed when necessary.

3   Tell someone you are going for a walk and your expected time of return.

4   Walk steadily. Let your arms swing, get a rhythm going.

5   If you are embarking on a long or strenuous walk, drink water before you start and carry some with you. A small backpack can carry your water, sunscreen, hat and glasses. Keep it stocked and ready to go.

6   If breathing becomes uncomfortable, slow down (don't come to a sudden stop: a sudden halt can cause dizziness).

7   In wintertime, a hat keeps you warm all over because one-third of our body heat is lost through the head.

8   Avoid walking immediately after meals (give it 15 minutes), or if you have a fever or bad cold.

9   If you are walking in the dark, wear light-coloured clothing so that you can be seen by motorists.

10   You may feel some soreness to begin with, but don't be worried. Your body will adapt and the soreness will decrease. Stretching for 2 minutes before and after will help minimise aches and pains.

Staying motivated

- Walk with a regular partner or group.
- Plan your walk in advance: will it be an early morning or late evening stroll?
- Vary your walking location.
- Visit national parks and landmarks.
- Walk the dog at a regular time each day—they'll soon start to remind you.
- Don't let rain put you off—take the umbrella, enjoy the sound of the rain.

Walking after heart surgery or heart attack

If you have recently had a heart attack or surgery, exercise will play an important role in your recovery. Walking is safe and easy, and you can begin an easy 5- to 10-minute stroll twice a day during the week you leave hospital. Build up gradually over 6 weeks to a 30-minute comfortable walk. Talk it over with your doctor first.

Chapter 9

The New Glucose Revolution Life Plan Menus

To show you how the many different aspects of nutrition can fit together to create a low GI way of living, we've designed some typical healthy menus. You'll find an emphasis on low GI carbohydrates along with plenty of fruit and vegetables, lean meats and seafood and healthy oils.

We've deliberately left quantities off most of the menus because it is not our intention to prescribe an amount of food to you (particularly considering we don't even know you!). We all have different energy needs and appetites—needs that vary from day to day—and consequently the amount of food we eat usually varies from day to day. This is normal and beneficial, particularly if our food choices reflect a similar variety.

If you would like more specific guidance with your diet we suggest you see an Accredited Practising Dietitian—check with your local hospital or look in the Yellow Pages under 'Dietitians'. Look for the letters 'APD' after their name, which

indicate that the practitioner has the qualifications and expertise to provide expert nutritional and dietary advice.

The 4 GI menus

1 FOR EVERYBODY

2 FOR BIGGERBODIES

3 FOR BUSYBODIES

4 FOR KIDSBODIES

There are four different types of menu, with slight modifications according to the expected user:

FOR EVERYBODY

These menus are designed for the average adult. They are also suitable for people with type 1 diabetes, with the inclusion of snacks.

FOR BIGGERBODIES

These menus have been modified for people trying to lose weight, including those with type 2 diabetes. The emphasis is on a moderate carbohydrate intake, to satisfy appetite, with a small amount of fat to save on kilojoules. If appetite is not a problem you may choose to use the menus for EveryBody, which are slightly higher in fat, but to lose weight you will need to moderate serve size or the kilojoule intake could be excessive.

FOR KIDSBODIES

These menus have been modified for children. Children are best fed a nourishing mix of carbohydrates and fats. The children's menus include variations on the dishes in the adult menus, with the inclusion of healthy snacks. Many of the snack foods children eat are high in fat and quickly digested, high GI carbohydrate, which may increase their risk of obesity. We suggest some healthier alternatives.

GETTING YOUR KIDS TO EAT SOMETHING DIFFERENT

Children are born with a liking for sweet tastes but they also prefer what they are familiar with. Initial rejection of a new food can eventually turn to acceptance if children are given lots of opportunities to sample the new food in a favourable environment. A small taste is all it takes, but changes in taste do occur gradually so 8 to 10 small tastes may be required.

DRINKS FOR CHILDREN

Offer children water to drink with their meals and limit the amount of cordial and soft drink they have. Around 200 ml of fruit juice and 400 ml of milk a day is sufficient for school-age children.

FOR BUSYBODIES

These menus have been modified for very active people. Active people need a high carbohydrate intake to fuel their muscles, but this needn't all be low GI. So in these menus you'll find large quantities of carbohydrate of different types. We've indicated the GI ranking of the carbohydrate in these menus and offer the following tips on when to use high and low GI carbohydrates for best performance.

USING THE GI TO BOOST YOUR SPORTS PERFORMANCE

Scientific research has so far identified 3 key applications of the GI to enhance sports performance:

1. Use high GI foods after exercise, in the recovery phase to enhance glycogen replenishment.

2. Use high GI foods or fluids during exercise to maintain blood glucose levels.

3. A low GI pre-event meal may enhance endurance in prolonged exercise.

BREAKFAST FOODS

FRUITS/JUICES

Fresh melon or pineapple, citrus fruits or juices, fresh strawberries, bananas, canned peaches or fresh nectarines, soft-cooked pears or apples

LOW FAT MILK

Including milk products such as low fat yoghurts and drinking yoghurt

LOW GI CEREALS

Oats, mueslis, All Bran™ and varieties, oat or rice bran

LOW GI BREADS

Wholegrain breads such as Bürgen™, Ploughman's Wholegrain™, Performax™, sourdough

LIGHT MEALS

VEGETABLES

Various salad greens, sprouts, cucumber, tomato, capsicum, celery, grated carrot, beetroot, canned corn, shallots, parsley and other fresh herbs

LOW GI BREADS

Wholegrain breads and rolls such as Bürgen™ , Ploughman's Wholegrain™, Performax™, sourdough

CEREALS AND GRAINS

Cracked wheat for tabbouleh, pasta or noodles

BEANS AND PULSES

Baked beans on toast, canned beans in a salad, split peas in soup, chickpeas in hummus

FISH

Canned tuna or salmon as part of a salad or sandwich

DAIRY FOODS

Eggs or cheese could make a change for one or two meals each week. Choose low fat cheeses such as ricotta or cottage, or look for low fat varieties of feta, cheddar or processed cheese

LEAN MEATS

Leg ham, pastrami, chicken breast

FRUITS

Avocado, olives, bananas, apples, grapes, kiwi-fruit. Look to buy whichever is the best quality for the best price. This should indicate that it is in season

MAIN MEALS

VEGETABLES

Remember we're aiming for at least 5 servings a day. Include a salad every day and use as wide a variety as possible of other vegetables (something green included!).

CEREALS AND GRAINS

Pasta, rice, noodles, couscous, polenta, barley

BEANS AND PULSES

Make it vegetarian at least once a week and try out a new recipe for pulses. Keep canned or Quickpulse™ varieties in the cupboard for a quick meal base.

FISH

Aim to include it twice a week or more using fresh or canned varieties.

DAIRY FOODS

Eggs make a quick protein option for a main meal that you may include once a week. Consider an omelette with vegetables, a souffle or simply poached eggs with slow roasted tomatoes, mushrooms and baked beans.

LEAN MEATS

Include lean red meat once or twice a week. Look for names such as 'Trim Lamb', 'New Fashioned Pork' and 'Master Trim Beef' when shopping for meat as a guide to the leanest cuts or ask your butcher for the leanest he has.

POULTRY

Use skinless chicken once a week. Skinless breast is the lowest in saturated fat.

FRUITS

Fresh fruit is the ideal end to a meal. Buying a selection of different fruits and slicing them up to make an attractive fruit platter encourages fruit consumption. When fresh is not looking the best, consider including some dried fruits (figs, apples, pears, apricots, raisins) on the platter with a small bowl of nuts. Also try canned and frozen fruits.

7-DAY LIFE PLAN MENUS

AN ASTERISK* NEXT TO A MEAL INDICATES THAT THE RECIPE IS INCLUDED IN THIS BOOK.

for everybody

MONDAY

BREAKFAST
Bürgen™ toast with avocado, sliced tomato and black pepper
Fresh citrus fruit or juice

LUNCH
Minestrone soup with a crusty bread roll
Low fat yoghurt and berries

DINNER
Deep sea bream fillets with semi-dried tomato marinade*,
Doongara rice, green bean, rocket and baby tomato salad*

TUESDAY

BREAKFAST
Swiss natural muesli topped with low fat yoghurt and sliced banana or berries
Apple juice

LUNCH
A mixed Mediterranean salad of lettuce, tomato, cucumber, capsicum, olives and sprouts with balsamic dressing* served with chunky oven-baked sweet potato wedges* and guacamole
A bunch of grapes

DINNER
Grilled fish fillet* or basted chicken breast served with sweet potato, potato and garlic mash*, spinach and snow peas

WEDNESDAY

BREAKFAST
Semolina and low fat milk flavoured with honey and vanilla
Plate of fresh melon slices: rockmelon, watermelon, honeydew
Low fat hot chocolate

LUNCH
Low GI bread with sardine toast topper* served with lettuce, sliced cucumber, shredded carrot and beetroot, and sprouts

DINNER
Vegetable and noodle stir-fry*
Rhubarb with honey and strawberries topped with natural yoghurt and a sprinkle of toasted walnuts

THURSDAY

BREAKFAST	LUNCH	DINNER
Poached egg with slow roasted tomatoes* and wholegrain toast Fresh grapefruit or juice	Toasted Turkish bread with hummus* and tabbouleh Sliced kiwi-fruit and banana	Pork fillet with spiced pears and Basmati rice* served with steamed carrot and zucchini or other fresh vegetables

FRIDAY

BREAKFAST	LUNCH	DINNER
Sautéed mushrooms, shallots and parsley served on wholegrain toast Tomato juice	Sourdough rye with lean roast beef and horseradish or smoked salmon and light cream cheese and capers Fresh fruit or juice	Mediterranean lasagne* with green salad Peaches and lite ice-cream

SATURDAY

BREAKFAST	LUNCH	DINNER
Wholegrain toast with peanut butter or Vegemite Orange juice	Omega-enriched salmon omelette* with wholegrain bread and salad greens	Butter bean, capsicum and prawn pilaf* Diced nectarine and banana topped with low fat fruit yoghurt and a sprinkle of toasted almonds

SUNDAY

BREAKFAST	LUNCH	DINNER
All Bran™ Soy 'n' Fibre with low fat milk or yoghurt and fresh or canned fruit	Chargrilled vegetables and beans with pasta* and a mixed green salad with olive oil vinaigrette Fresh fruit	Lean lamb roast brushed with oil, rosemary and dried mint, baked over water, served with chargrilled garlic potatoes and sweet potato* and fresh steamed greens Individual apple and ginger crumble*

7-DAY LIFE PLAN MENUS

AN ASTERISK* NEXT TO A MEAL INDICATES THAT THE RECIPE IS INCLUDED IN THIS BOOK.

for biggerbodies

MONDAY

BREAKFAST
2 slices wholegrain toast spread with ½ an avocado and topped with sliced tomato and black pepper
Grapefruit or tomato juice

LUNCH
Hearty winter vegetable soup* with a wholegrain roll and a small apple

DINNER
Deep sea bream fillets with semi-dried tomato marinade* served with ½ cup of Doongara rice, and green bean, rocket and baby tomato salad*

TUESDAY

BREAKFAST
Natural muesli (about ½ cup) with Shape™ yoghurt and fresh strawberries

LUNCH
A mixed salad of cherry tomatoes, chopped cucumber and celery, baby beets, marinated mushrooms and mesclun lettuce with a cornmeal, capsicum and chive muffin*

DINNER
Grilled fish fillet* or basted chicken breast (120 g) served with sweet potato, potato and garlic mash*, spinach and snow peas

WEDNESDAY

BREAKFAST
⅓ cup of raw rolled oats and a tablespoon of raisins with low fat milk
Fresh grapefruit

LUNCH
Ricotta, avocado and sprout* open sandwich
Sliced rockmelon

DINNER
Vegetable and noodle stir-fry*
Rhubarb with honey and strawberries topped with a dollop of low fat plain yoghurt

7-DAY LIFE PLAN MENUS

THURSDAY

BREAKFAST
Multigrain toast with a smear of canola margarine, Vegemite and a boiled egg
Tomato or orange juice

LUNCH
Toasted Turkish bread with hummus* and tabbouleh
Sliced kiwi-fruit

DINNER
Pork fillet with spiced pears* and ½ cup of Basmati rice served with steamed carrot and zucchini or other fresh vegetables

FRIDAY

BREAKFAST
Sautéed mushrooms with chopped parsley and shallots, seasoned with soy sauce, served with 2 slices Performax™ toast
Skim milk cappuccino

LUNCH
A sandwich of low GI bread filled with salmon and lemon juice, lettuce and tomato
Fresh fruit

DINNER
Mediterranean lasagne* with green salad
Peaches and a scoop of lite ice-cream

SATURDAY

BREAKFAST
2 slices of wholegrain toast spread with canola margarine and Vegemite or marmalade
Small glass of orange juice

LUNCH
Combine leftover pasta with a can of tuna, chopped tomato, celery, cucumber and parsley; dress with balsamic vinaigrette* or a dessertspoon of canola mayonnaise

DINNER
Butter bean, capsicum and prawn pilaf*
Diced nectarine with a dollop of low fat vanilla yoghurt and a slice of crisp almond bread

SUNDAY

BREAKFAST
½ cup of All Bran™ Soy 'n' Fibre with low fat milk or yoghurt topped with ½ cup fresh or canned peach slices or berries

LUNCH
Chickpea, tomato and eggplant* with toasted bread and a mixed green salad with olive oil vinaigrette

DINNER
Lean lamb roast brushed with oil, rosemary and dried mint and baked over water, served with chargrilled garlic potatoes and sweet potato* and fresh steamed greens
Fresh fruit plate

7-DAY LIFE PLAN MENUS

AN ASTERISK* NEXT TO A MEAL INDICATES THAT THE RECIPE IS INCLUDED IN THIS BOOK.

for kidsbodies

MONDAY

BREAKFAST
Banana smoothie with vanilla yoghurt, honey and wheatgerm

SNACK
Raisin toast with canola margarine

LUNCH
Ham sandwich with cherry tomatoes
Small apple and mini yoghurt

SNACK
Frozen orange quarters

DINNER
Barbecued chicken with corn cobs and salad
Trim custard served over canned pear halves

TUESDAY

BREAKFAST
An apricot and muesli muffin* and a bowl of fruit salad with yoghurt

SNACK
A bag of home-popped popcorn

LUNCH
Wholemeal lavash bread topped with hummus, shredded lettuce, cheese, tuna and carrot
Sliced fresh apple

SNACK
Toast with Vegemite

DINNER
Oven-fried fish with chunky chips. Choose products cooked in canola oil. Offer fresh raw vegetable sticks alongside
Stewed apples with low fat vanilla yoghurt

WEDNESDAY

BREAKFAST
Low GI toast with peanut butter, honey and sliced banana

SNACK
Milk and Milo™

LUNCH
Low GI toast topped with creamed corn, mushroom and melted cheese

SNACK
Crumpet and honey

DINNER
'Home-made' chicken and noodle soup: add slivers of chicken and pasta to salt-reduced packet mix. Boil 10 minutes. Add mixed frozen vegies and chopped shallots near the end of cooking
Top canned fruit with muesli and bake in moderate oven for 10 minutes. Serve with low fat vanilla yoghurt

THURSDAY

BREAKFAST
Nutri-Grain™ with milk and sliced banana
SNACK
Snack pack of peaches

LUNCH
Jacket potato topped with beans and cheese
SNACK
Chopped strawberries, banana, grapes and peach with fruit yoghurt

DINNER
Fish and vegetable kebabs. with pineapple pieces, button mushrooms and cherry tomatoes. Grill, basting with a mix of oil, soy sauce and warmed honey. Serve with noodles or rice

FRIDAY

BREAKFAST
Baked beans on toast
Fresh fruit
SNACK
A slice of cheese and wholemeal crackers

LUNCH
Salmon and lettuce on Performax™ low GI bread
SNACK
Fruit yoghurt
Choc chip cookies

DINNER
Mediterranean lasagne*
Fresh strawberries with a scoop of lite ice-cream

SATURDAY

BREAKFAST
Porridge with low fat milk, sultanas and juice
SNACK
2 oatmeal biscuits* and a glass of milk

LUNCH
Tuna, chopped celery and mayonnaise roll
Fruit juice
SNACK
Vegetable strips with corn relish and cottage cheese dip

DINNER
Vegetable and noodle stir-fry*
Lite ice-cream with sliced banana, nuts and chocolate syrup

SUNDAY

BREAKFAST
Mini-Wheats™ with low fat milk
A slice of raisin toast
Hot chocolate
SNACK
Paddle-Pop™

LUNCH
Spaghetti or pasta twists with basic tomato sauce*
A bowl of small chunks of fresh fruit offered with toothpicks and yoghurt to dip.
SNACK
Cheese and fruit plate with water crackers

DINNER
Lean lamb roast with potato and sweet potato chunks, peas and mint sauce

AN ASTERISK* NEXT TO A MEAL INDICATES THAT THE RECIPE IS INCLUDED IN THIS BOOK.

for busybodies

We have indicated the GI rating of the carbohydrate foods in the following meals and snacks to help you choose the right type of food for your circumstances.

Δ = High GI carbohydrate   ‡ = Low GI carbohydrate

MONDAY

BREAKFAST	LUNCH	DINNER
4 slices wholegrain fruit and nut loaf‡, toasted and topped with light cream cheese, slices of apple‡, and cinnamon	2 sandwiches on mixed grain bread‡ with tuna, tomato, onion, cucumber	Garlic prawns, capsicum and coriander pasta*‡, green salad and bread roll
A glass of low fat milk‡	A banana and fruit juice‡	Fresh fruit‡

TUESDAY

BREAKFAST	LUNCH	DINNER
Large serve of chunky fresh fruit salad‡ topped with light yoghurt‡ and low fat toasted muesli‡	Lavash bread with lettuce, tomato, grated cheese and canned Mexican beans	Roasted sweet potato, garlic and rosemary pilaf*‡
Apricot and muesli muffin	An apple‡	Summer pudding*‡
	Low fat flavoured milk‡	

WEDNESDAY

BREAKFAST	LUNCH	DINNER
Rolled oats‡ cooked with mixed dried fruit‡, topped with pecans or walnuts	3 sandwiches with lean roast meat and salad	Antipasto (vegetarian) with bread
Toast with honeyΔ	Juice‡	Vegetarian pizza
Low fat milk or juice‡		GelatoΔ

THURSDAY

BREAKFAST
Banana and honey jaffles made with Performax™ bread‡. (Use a light spread of canola margarine.)
Skim milk cappuccino‡

LUNCH
Beef and lentil burgers‡ on a toasted wholemeal rollΔ, served with mixed lettuce, sliced tomato and chilli sauce
Flavoured mineral waterΔ

DINNER
Warm lamb salad* with 2 bread rolls
Poached pears‡ with low fat vanilla yoghurt‡ and toasted flaked almonds

FRIDAY

BREAKFAST
Baked bean and light cheese melts on Performax™ bread‡
Canned peach slices‡

LUNCH
Vegetable and rice noodle‡ Vietnamese soup
Fruit salad‡

DINNER
Vegetable bake with a bread rollΔ
Fresh rockmelonΔ with lite ice-cream‡

SATURDAY

BREAKFAST
4 slices Performax™ toast‡ with peanut butter and honey
Orange juice‡

LUNCH
Marinated BBQ chicken noodle salad*‡
Canned fruit‡

DINNER
Thai green chicken curry* with Doongara rice‡
Mango lassi‡

SUNDAY

BREAKFAST
Just Right™ topped with a sliced banana, low fat milk
A couple of slices of wholegrain toast‡ with jam
An apple and fruit juice‡

LUNCH
Spaghetti‡ with basic tomato sauce
Bread rollΔ and fruit juice‡

DINNER
Seared tuna steaks with red capsicum sauce, Doongara rice‡
Fresh fruit platter‡

SNACKS

Dried fruit and nut mix‡
Raisin toast‡
Fresh fruit‡
Low fat milk with chocolate flavouring‡
Low fat yoghurt‡

A fruit smoothie‡
Muffins (see our recipes)
Snack packs of canned fruit‡
Scones and jamΔ
Banana sandwichΔ
Creamed rice

Sustagen™ ‡
PancakesΔ
PikeletsΔ
Breakfast barsΔ
Toast and honeyΔ
Bowl of Nutri-Grain™

IN THE PANTRY

Dried herbs and spices

Whole black peppercorns

Chilli powder

Ground cumin and coriander

Prepared mustard, e.g. Dijon and wholegrain

OILS AND VINEGARS

Extra virgin olive oil

Mustard seed oil

Canola oil

Sunola™

Sesame oil

White wine vinegar

Red wine vinegar

Balsamic vinegar

GRAIN FOODS

Pasta and noodles (fresh and dried)

Doongara and Basmati rice

Couscous

Polenta (cornmeal)

Pearl barley or Barley Quick™

Cracked wheat (bulgur)

PULSES AND BEANS

Vacuum packed beans and pulses (Quickpulse™)

Canned of all types

Dried lentils and split peas

SAUCES

Soy sauce

Oyster sauce

Fish sauce

Chinese rice wine

Chilli sauce

Bottled tomato pasta sauce

Curry pastes

BOTTLED FOODS

Sundried tomatoes

Artichoke hearts

Olives

Capers

Marinated feta cheese

Marinated vegetables

CANNED FOOD

Tuna in springwater, brine, or oil

Salmon in springwater or brine

Sardines in springwater, brine, oil or tomato sauce

Tomatoes and tomato paste

Sweetcorn

Light coconut milk

Fruits

Note Fish canned in oil contains about 10 times more fat than fish canned in water. If you prefer to buy tuna in oil, check the ingredient list closely for the type of oil used: canola or olive are best.

NUTS, SEEDS AND DRIED FRUIT

Almonds, walnuts, pinenuts, pecans, sultanas, raisins, apricots

Pepitas, sesame seeds, sunflower seeds, linseeds

IN THE FRIDGE

Omega-enriched eggs

Low fat or skim milk

Canola margarine

Canola mayonnaise

Parmesan cheese

Ricotta cheese

Reduced fat cheddar

Low fat natural and fruit yoghurt

Fresh pasta, hokkien noodles

Fresh vegetables, including green leafy vegetables: lettuce, spinach, Asian greens, cabbage, broccoli

Lemons

Onions

Tomatoes

Fresh herbs such as parsley and basil

Ginger, garlic, chilli: bottled or fresh

Note If you buy fresh ginger and need to keep it more than a week, peel it, place in a jar, cover with oil and refrigerate; or peel, place in a freezer bag and freeze.

IN THE FREEZER

Peas, beans

Frozen spinach

Mixed vegetables

Reduced fat ice-cream or sorbet

Frozen berries

50
Life Plan
recipes

PART THREE

Chapter 10: **About the Recipes**

Chapter 11: **Snacks, Soups and Salads**

Chapter 12: **Pasta, Noodles and Grains**

Chapter 13: **Mains and Accompaniments**

Chapter 14: **Desserts**

About the Recipes

Our recipes are based on a dietary philosophy that includes an emphasis on:

- low GI carbohydrate, with carbohydrate meeting 40 to 50 per cent of energy requirements
- monounsaturated fats and omega-3 fats, with 30 to 35 per cent of energy coming from fat
- a moderate level of protein providing 15 to 20 per cent of energy

Major ingredients are fish and seafood, legumes, whole grains, olive oil and fresh fruit and vegetables.

Nutrition information

Nutrition information has been included with each recipe. This includes details of the energy (kilojoules/calories), protein, fat, carbohydrate and fibre content per serve. Where there is a range in the number of serves the recipe yields, the nutrition information relates to the larger number of servings.

Energy requirements

In keeping with our dietary philosophy, we recommend the following levels of macronutrients for various energy requirements. (These energy levels are an approximate guide only, and assume good health status and a moderate level of activity.)

An average energy requirement for young to middle-aged men: 10 000 kilojoules/2400 calories, made up of 90 to 120 grams protein, 80 to 110 grams fat, 250 to 315 grams carbohydrate

An average energy requirement for young to middle-aged women and older men, and a reduced energy intake for younger men: 8400 kilojoules/2000 calories made up of 75 to 100 grams protein, 70 to 90 grams fat, 210 to 265 grams carbohydrate

An average energy requirement for older women, a reduced energy intake for young to middle-aged women, and a low energy intake for men: 6300 kilojoules/1500 calories made up of 55 to 75 grams protein, 50 to 70 grams fat, 160 to 200 grams carbohydrate

A low energy intake for young to middle-aged women: 5000 kilojoules/1200 calories made up of 45 to 60 grams protein, 40 to 55 grams fat, 125 to 160 grams carbohydrate

Fat

The emphasis is on minimising saturated fat and increasing unsaturated fat. We've made a particular effort to increase omega-3 fats in the recipes and use omega neutral monounsaturates. The amount of long chain omega-3 marine equivalent has been estimated for each recipe and indicated with a star rating that reflects the quantity per serve.

Those of you who have been following a low fat diet may be surprised by the fat content of some of the recipes. Dietary guidelines are changing. There is a move away from very low fat diets as science reveals the health benefits of certain types of fats. It is important, however, to remember that an increase in fat intake will result in an increase in kilojoule intake unless a compensatory reduction in another nutrient, such as carbohydrate, is made.

Because of this, we feel that a higher fat diet will not suit everyone. In particular, those people who have a big appetite and like to eat a large volume of food could control their weight more easily on a low fat,

OMEGA-3 RATING

>1000 milligrams per serve	*****	One of the richest sources of omega-3
500–1000 milligrams per serve	****	A very good source of omega-3
100–500 milligrams per serve	***	A good source of omega-3
50–100 milligrams per serve	**	Valuable amounts of omega-3
<50 milligrams per serve	*	A small amount of omega-3

The absence of an omega-3 rating signifies there is negligible omega-3 content in that recipe. Saturated fat provides less than 10 per cent of the energy content of all recipes except where specifically stated otherwise in the nutrient information.

high carbohydrate diet. Low fat, high carbohydrate foods are less energy dense than higher fat foods, which means that it is possible to eat a larger volume of them while still eating within energy requirements.

If you are trying to lose weight, and struggle with hunger sometimes, work on keeping to the lower fat intakes for various energy levels recommended above. For example, for a young to middle-aged woman on a reduced kilojoule intake of about 6300 kilojoules/1500 calories, aiming for around 50 grams of fat per day allows a more generous amount of carbohydrate in the diet at 200 grams per day.

Carbohydrate

Many of the recipes are carbohydrate-based, but the emphasis is on low GI carbohydrate. Each recipe bears the 'G' symbol and has an accompanying GI ranking according to whether its GI is low, intermediate or high. The following table gives approximate GI values for these different rankings.

Recipes that are low in carbohydrate have little effect on our blood glucose levels, so we have given them a GI rating of zero.

GI RATING
Ⓖ low = a GI of less than 55
Ⓖ moderate = a GI of 56–69
Ⓖ high = a GI greater than 70

Protein

There is evidence that humans evolved on much higher protein intakes than we eat today, although as yet there is insufficient evidence to suggest that we need to greatly increase our protein intakes. Protein foods are a critical source of some nutrients such as iron (from red meat) and omega-3 fats (from fish and seafood). Most people consume 15 to 20 per cent of energy as protein, which is in line with current guidelines. The protein content of the recipes varies according to the main ingredients, with main meal dishes, based on meat, fish or legumes, being higher in protein than recipes based entirely on vegetables.

Fibre

A diet rich in fruit and vegetables will be naturally high in fibre. On Western diets most people are lucky to consume 20 grams of fibre a day, when recommendations are that we eat 30 grams or more. The daily fibre requirements of children and adolescents are estimated as their age in years plus five: this gives the number of grams of fibre recommended per day.

Most of the recipes in this book are high in fibre, providing an average of 5 grams of fibre per serve.

Chapter 11

Snacks, Soups and Salads

Capsicum, Corn and Barley Patties

500 g sweet potato, peeled

1 cup (60 g) quick cook/instant barley (from health food stores)

1 x 420 g can corn kernels, drained

1 red capsicum (approx. 200 g), halved, seeded and diced small

½ bunch flat leafed or curly parsley, finely chopped (approx. ½ cup)

1 x 60 g omega-enriched egg, lightly beaten

salt and freshly ground black pepper

2 tablespoons canola oil

1. Cut the sweet potato into chunks and boil in plenty of water till soft. Drain, mash till smooth, and place in a large mixing bowl.

2. Add the raw barley, drained corn kernels, diced capsicum and chopped parsley. Blend in the beaten egg with a large spoon, and season with salt and freshly ground pepper.

3. Heat the oil in a heavy-based frying pan. Shape the patties with wetted hands, and cook for 5 minutes, turning once only, till golden brown.

Makes 8 large or 12 small patties   Preparation time: 10 minutes   Cooking time: 20 minutes

Ⓖ **LOW**   OMEGA-3 **

| kJ/cal **473/113** | PROTEIN **3g** | FAT **4g** | CARBOHYDRATE **15g** | FIBRE **3g** |

Cornmeal, Capsicum and Chive Muffins

3 tablespoons canola oil
2 tablespoons honey
1½ cups (375 ml) buttermilk
1 x 60 g omega-enriched egg
1 x 400 g can corn kernels, drained
1 red capsicum (approx. 150 g), finely diced
1 bunch chives, snipped
1 cup (180 g) cornmeal/polenta
1½ cups (185 g) self-raising flour
pinch salt

1. Preheat the oven to 190°C.

2. Lightly oil a 12-hole muffin tray.

3. In a large mixing bowl, beat together the oil, honey, buttermilk and egg. Add the corn kernels, diced capsicum and chives, then quickly stir in the cornmeal, flour and salt.

4. Spoon the muffin mixture into the prepared tins, and bake for 25 to 30 minutes, till cooked through and golden brown.

Makes 12 ▪ Preparation time: 20 minutes ▪ Cooking time: 30 minutes

Ⓖ **MODERATE**   OMEGA-3 **

| kJ/cal 864/206 | PROTEIN 6g | FAT 7g | CARBOHYDRATE 30g | FIBRE 2g |

Apricot and Muesli Muffins

1 cup (170 g) plump dried apricots, coarsely chopped

1½ cups (170 g) unsweetened natural muesli

2 cups (250 g) self-raising flour

1 teaspoon baking powder

1 cup (250 ml) apple juice

3 tablespoons canola oil

¼ cup (100 ml) honey

1 x 60 g omega-enriched egg

1. Preheat the oven to 190°C.

2. Lightly oil a 12-hole muffin tray.

3. In a large mixing bowl mix together the chopped apricots, muesli, self-raising flour and baking powder.

4. In another bowl combine the apple juice, oil, honey and egg. Add the flour mixture to the liquid mix and stir till just combined.

5. Spoon the muffin mixture into the prepared muffin tins and bake for 20 minutes, till brown and cooked through.

Makes 12 ⁿ Preparation time: 10 minutes ⁿ Cooking time: 20 minutes

Ⓖ **MODERATE**   OMEGA-3 **

| kJ/cal 990/237 | PROTEIN 5g | FAT 7g | CARBOHYDRATE 38g | FIBRE 4g |

Choc Chip Muffins

1 cup (150 g) wholemeal self-raising flour
1 cup (150 g) self-raising flour
1 cup (240 g) dark brown sugar, lightly packed
1 tablespoon mixed spice
1 cup (200 g) choc chips
1 cup (250 ml) buttermilk
1 teaspoon vanilla essence
2 x 60 g omega-enriched eggs
1 tablespoon canola oil

1. Preheat the oven to 190°C and lightly oil a 12-hole muffin tray.

2. In one bowl mix together the flours, sugar and mixed spice. Fold in the choc chips.

3. In another large mixing bowl whisk together the buttermilk, vanilla essence, eggs and canola oil.

4. Quickly stir the dry ingredients into the buttermilk mixture and spoon into the prepared muffin tray.

5. Place in the preheated oven and bake for 25 minutes, till well risen, brown and cooked through.

Makes 12 " Preparation time: 10 minutes " Cooking time: 25 minutes

Ⓖ **MODERATE**   OMEGA-3 **

| kJ/cal | 1170/280 | PROTEIN | 7g | FAT | 8g | CARBOHYDRATE | 46g | FIBRE | 2g |

Chargrilled Vegetables and Beans with Pasta, page 177

Turkish Hummus

1 x 400 g can chickpeas
½ cup (130 g) tahini (sesame seed paste)
2 cloves garlic, coarsely chopped
1/3 cup (80 ml) lemon juice
salt and freshly ground black pepper

1. Drain the chickpeas and reserve the liquid.

2. In a food processor, combine the chickpeas, tahini paste, garlic, lemon juice and seasonings. Process, adding enough reserved chickpea liquid to make a smooth consistency.

3. Serve with a low GI bread as a dip, in place of butter in sandwiches, or layered with chargrilled vegetables on focaccia.

Makes 2 cups ″ Preparation time: 15 minutes ″ NOTE Nutrition information below is for ¼ cup.

Ⓖ **LOW**   OMEGA-3 *

| kJ/cal **558/133** | PROTEIN **6g** | FAT **10g** | CARBOHYDRATE **4g** | FIBRE **4g** |

Chicken, Avocado, Sprout and Ricotta Bake

(Although this recipe is high in fat, 70 per cent of the fat is unsaturated)

4 slices Performax™ bread
½ cup (60 g) reduced fat ricotta cheese
1 cooked chicken breast, sliced
½ punnet mung bean sprouts
1 large, ripe avocado, sliced
salt and freshly ground black pepper

1. Toast one side of the four bread slices.

2. Spread the other side with the ricotta cheese, and top with sliced chicken breast, sprouts and sliced avocado. Grind a generous amount of salt and pepper over the open sandwiches.

3. Place under a preheated grill and cook for 3 minutes.

4. Serve hot for a quick snack.

Serves 2

Ⓖ **LOW**   OMEGA-3 *

| kJ/cal 2504/596 | PROTEIN 32g | FAT 38g | CARBOHYDRATE 33g | FIBRE 10g |

Baby Pea and Ham Soup

1 large smoked ham bone

2 litres water

4 large carrots (approx. 700 g), diced

4 celery stalks, diced

3 large onions (approx. 500 g), finely diced

3 bay leaves

500 g packet frozen baby peas

½ bunch parsley, coarsely chopped

freshly ground black pepper

1. Place the ham bone and water in a large saucepan and bring to the boil. Remove any froth that forms on the surface. Simmer for 5 minutes, then add the prepared carrots, celery, onions and bay leaves.

2. Simmer gently for 40 minutes, removing any scum as it appears. Remove the bone from the water, cut off any meat and dice. Discard the fat and skin.

3. Return the diced ham to the saucepan and add the peas, simmering gently till tender.

4. Add the chopped parsley, season with pepper and serve hot with thick slices of low GI toast.

Serves 6 ▪ Preparation time: 10 minutes ▪ Cooking time: 50 minutes

Ⓖ LOW

kJ/cal **508/121**	PROTEIN **12g**	FAT **1g**	CARBOHYDRATE **15g**	FIBRE **10g**

Sweet Potato, Carrot and Ginger Soup

1 kg sweet potato, peeled and cut into large pieces

1 kg carrots, peeled and cut into large pieces

1 large brown onion (approx. 200 g), peeled and quartered

2 cloves garlic, peeled and coarsely chopped

4 cups (1 litre) chicken stock

1 stalk lemongrass, cut into 3 pieces

200 ml low fat (lite) coconut cream

200 ml water

1 x 2 cm piece fresh ginger, peeled and finely chopped

salt and freshly ground black pepper

coriander leaves

1. Place the prepared sweet potato, carrots, onion and garlic into a large saucepan or stockpot.

2. Add the chicken stock and lemongrass pieces and simmer till the vegetables are soft. Remove the lemongrass pieces, add the coconut cream, water and chopped ginger, and cook for a further 5 minutes.

3. Puree the soup till smooth, season to taste with salt and pepper and garnish with coriander leaves. Serve hot with slices of Bürgen™ Oatbran bread.

Serves 6 ⁄ Preparation time: 10 minutes ⁄ Cooking time: 25 minutes

Ⓖ LOW

| kJ/cal 823/196 | PROTEIN 5g | FAT 5g | CARBOHYDRATE 33g | FIBRE 9g |

Hearty Winter Vegetable Soup

1 x 400 g can green lentils, drained

4 cups (1 litre) chicken stock

1 large leek, washed and finely sliced

½ bunch celery, finely sliced

1 x 800 g can whole peeled tomatoes, undrained

1 x 420 g can tomato puree

salt and freshly ground black pepper

½ bunch flat leafed parsley, coarsely chopped

60 g parmesan cheese, shaved from the block

1. Combine the lentils, chicken stock, sliced leek, celery, tomatoes and juice, tomato puree and a grinding of salt and pepper in a large saucepan or stockpot.

2. Bring to the boil then simmer for 15 minutes. Stir in the coarsely chopped parsley and ladle into soup bowls.

3. Sprinkle each bowl with the shaved parmesan and serve with thick slices of low GI toast.

Serves 8 " Preparation time: 5 minutes " Cooking time: 15 minutes

 LOW   OMEGA-3 *

| kJ/cal **430/102** | PROTEIN **8g** | FAT **3g** | CARBOHYDRATE **11g** | FIBRE **5g** |

Roast Chicken, Garlic and Borlotti Bean Soup

6 whole cloves garlic

1 roasted size 15 chicken (no stuffing)

2 litres low salt chicken stock or consomme

½ bunch thyme, leaves removed from stalks

zest of one lemon

2 small celery stalks, finely sliced

1 x 400 g can borlotti beans, drained

salt and freshly ground black pepper

half bunch flat leafed parsley, coarsely chopped

1. Preheat the oven to 180°C.

2. Prick each unpeeled clove of garlic with a sharp knife and place on a baking tray. Bake in preheated oven for 20 minutes. Remove, peel and mash.

3. Remove the skin from the chicken and cut the flesh (in small pieces) from the bones. Discard the carcass.

4. Pour stock into a large saucepan and add the roasted garlic mash, thyme leaves, lemon zest, celery, beans. Season with salt and pepper. Bring stock to the boil, simmer gently for 5 minutes, then add the chicken pieces.

5. Taste for flavour and serve with coarsely chopped parsley scattered over the top.

Serves 4–6 ″ Preparation time: 10 minutes ″ Cooking time: 25 minutes

Ⓖ **LOW**   OMEGA-3 **··**

| kJ/cal **1250/300** | PROTEIN **43g** | FAT **12g** | CARBOHYDRATE **7g** | FIBRE **5g** |

Pumpkin, Sweet Potato and Cumin Dhal Soup

2 kg pumpkin (Gramma or Jap)

2 large sweet potatoes (approx. 200 g each)

2 large red onions (approx. 200 g each)

2 cloves garlic

1 teaspoon canola oil

2 litres chicken stock

2 cups (400 g) dried red lentils

1 tablespoon cumin

salt and freshly ground black pepper

½ bunch flat leafed parsley

1. Peel and cut the pumpkin, sweet potato and onions into pieces. Finely chop the garlic.

2. Heat the oil in a large, heavy-based saucepan and toss the pumpkin, sweet potato, onions and garlic for 3 minutes over a moderate heat. Add the chicken stock, lentils and cumin, and simmer for 30 minutes or until the pumpkin is very soft.

3. Blend the contents together till smooth and season with a little salt and pepper. Reheat, garnish with coarsely chopped parsley, and serve with warm crusty bread.

Serves 4–6 ▪ Preparation time: 10 minutes ▪ Cooking time: 40 minutes

Ⓖ **LOW** OMEGA-3 **

| kJ/cal 1570/375 | PROTEIN 26g | FAT 5g | CARBOHYDRATE 57g | FIBRE 16g |

Chunky Vegetable, Chicken and Pasta Soup

2 litres chicken stock

4 carrots (approx. 500 g), diced

2 large sweet potatoes (approx. 200 g each), diced

2 large brown onions (approx. 400 g), diced

6 Brussels sprouts, cut in half

3 stalks celery, diced

1 x 400 g can corn niblets, drained

2 cups (200 g) spirali pasta

4 chicken thigh fillets, trimmed of all fat and sliced

4 stalks flat leafed parsley, coarsely chopped

salt and freshly ground black pepper

1. Prepare the vegetables and chicken.

2. Heat the chicken stock in a large saucepan.

3. Add the carrots, sweet potato and onions and simmer for 10 minutes. Add the corn niblets, Brussels sprouts, celery, pasta and chicken pieces and simmer gently for a further 10 minutes or until pasta is cooked.

4. Sprinkle with parsley and season to taste. Serve hot with Bürgen™ grain bread.

Serves 4-6 « Preparation time: 15 minutes « Cooking time: 20 minutes

Ⓖ LOW   OMEGA-3 ·

| kJ/cal **1456/347** | PROTEIN **23g** | FAT **4g** | CARBOHYDRATE **54g** | FIBRE **9g** |

Three Bean and Basil Salad

1 x 400 g can canellini beans, drained
1 x 400 g can borlotti beans, drained
1 x 400 g can red kidney beans, drained
2 cloves garlic, crushed
3 tablespoons extra virgin olive oil
1 tablespoon lemon juice
salt and freshly ground black pepper
½ bunch basil leaves, torn

1. Rinse all the drained beans well under cold running water. Drain.

2. Combine the beans in a large serving bowl or flat white platter.

3. In a lidded jar, combine the garlic, olive oil, lemon juice and seasonings and shake well.

4. Pour over the beans and toss through the basil leaves.

Serves 6–8 ≈ Preparation time: 5 minutes

 LOW   OMEGA-3 *

| kJ/cal 595/142 | PROTEIN 6g | FAT 8g | CARBOHYDRATE 13g | FIBRE 7g |

Roma Tomato, Mint and Cucumber Salad

(To accompany Mediterranean Lasagne, page 201)

10 (approx. 500 g) Roma tomatoes
2 tablespoons fresh mint, chopped
3–4 (approx. 500 g) Lebanese cucumbers
15 kalamata olives
30 g parmesan cheese, shaved from the block

DRESSING
10 mint leaves
3 tablespoons olive oil
3 tablespoons white wine vinegar
1 clove garlic, crushed
salt and freshly ground black pepper

1. Slice the Roma tomatoes crossways and sprinkle with chopped mint. Slice the cucumbers crossways and toss in a salad bowl with the tomatoes.

2. Add the olives and sprinkle with shaved parmesan cheese.

3. Combine the dressing ingredients in a blender, or chop the mint and combine in a screw-top jar and shake to mix. Pour over the salad and serve immediately.

Serves 6 ≈ Preparation time: 10 minutes

Ⓖ ZERO   OMEGA-3 ˙

| kJ/cal 566/135 | PROTEIN 3g | FAT 12g | CARBOHYDRATE 4g | FIBRE 3g |

Celery, Walnut and Lemon Thyme Salad

(To accompany Fresh Fettucine with Scallops, page 175)

½ bunch celery
100 g Californian walnuts
6 sprigs lemon thyme, leaves stripped from stalks

DRESSING
1 teaspoon celery seeds
1 tablespoon lemon juice
2 tablespoons apple juice
2 tablespoons extra virgin olive oil
1 tablespoon fresh thyme leaves
salt and freshly ground black pepper

1. Wash and slice the celery sticks diagonally.

2. In a salad bowl, toss the celery with whole walnuts and thyme sprigs.

3. Place all the dressing ingredients in a screw-top jar and shake.
Pour over the salad and serve with crusty low GI bread.

Serves 6 ▪ Preparation time: 10 minutes

 ZERO   OMEGA-3 ***

| kJ/cal 752/180 | PROTEIN 3g | FAT 18g | CARBOHYDRATE 3g | FIBRE 3g |

Green Bean, Rocket, Baby Tomato and Olive Salad

(To accompany Deep Sea Bream Fillets
with Semi-dried Tomato Marinade, page 200)

300 g green beans
1 bunch rocket lettuce
1 punnet (250 g) cherry tomatoes
3 green shallots, finely sliced
10 kalamata olives
6 basil leaves, torn

DRESSING
2 tablespoons wine vinegar
1/4 cup extra virgin olive oil
1 clove garlic, crushed
salt and freshly ground black pepper

1. Wash, top and tail the beans, and halve if very long. Wash the rocket and discard any unattractive leaves. Wash the tomatoes, halve half the tomatoes in the punnet, and combine all with the beans and rocket lettuce leaves on a white platter or in a shallow bowl.

2. Slice the shallots, and combine in a bowl with the olives and torn basil leaves. Scatter over the salad vegetables.

3. Place all the dressing ingredients into a screw-top jar and shake to mix.

4. Pour the dressing over the salad.

Serves 6 ▪ Preparation time: 15 minutes

(G) **ZERO**   OMEGA-3 *

| kJ/cal **465/110** | PROTEIN **2g** | FAT **10g** | CARBOHYDRATE **3g** | FIBRE **3g** |

Grilled Red Capsicum, Sweet Potato and Herb Salad

2 large red capsicum (approx. 200 g each), halved and seeded

4 medium sized sweet potatoes (approx. 150 g each), peeled

1 tablespoon mustard seed oil or olive oil

½ bunch chives, left whole

1 bunch flat leafed parsley, coarsely chopped

salt and freshly ground black pepper

1 tablespoon balsamic vinegar

1. Preheat the grill to high. Place the capsicum halves, skin side up, under the hot grill and cook till black blisters appear (approx. 10 mins). Place the capsicum into a paper bag. When cool, remove the skin and cut the flesh into thick slices.

2. Parboil the sweet potato (approx. 10 mins), drain and slice diagonally. Brush each wedge with mustard seed oil. Place on a sheet of foil under the grill and cook till golden brown (approx. 15 mins).

3. Arrange the capsicum strips and sweet potato slices on a platter or in a shallow bowl. Decorate with the herbs, sprinkle some salt and freshly ground black pepper over the vegetables, and drizzle with balsamic vinegar and any remaining oil.

4. Serve with crusty low GI rolls.

Serves 4 · Preparation time: 10 minutes · Cooking time: 25 minutes

Ⓖ **LOW**   OMEGA-3 **

| kJ/cal **698/166** | PROTEIN **5g** | FAT **5g** | CARBOHYDRATE **25g** | FIBRE **4g** |

Chapter 12

Pasta, Noodles and Grains

Fresh Fettucine with Scallops

500 g fresh fettucine

24 scallops with coral attached

4 cloves garlic, coarsely chopped

3 red chillies, seeded and coarsely chopped

1 bunch flat leafed parsley, coarsely chopped

1 tablespoon extra virgin olive oil

salt and freshly ground black pepper

1. Cook the pasta in rapidly boiling salted water for 3 minutes.

2. Combine the chopped garlic, chillies and parsley in a small bowl.

3. Heat the olive oil in a heavy-based frying pan and add the scallops, cooking for 2 minutes, turning once only. Remove from the pan.

4. Add the garlic, chillies and parsley to the pan and heat through. Add the drained pasta, add a grind of salt and black pepper, toss and serve immediately, topped with the cooked scallops.

Serves 4–6 ɴ Preparation time: 5 minutes ɴ Cooking time: 10 minutes

Ⓖ**LOW**   OMEGA-3 ***

| kJ/cal **659/157** | PROTEIN **10g** | FAT **4g** | CARBOHYDRATE **21g** | FIBRE **2g** |

Fettucine with Vegetables and Sausage

500 g spinach fettucine

1 teaspoon olive oil

2 brown onions (approx. 400 g), coarsely chopped

2 cloves garlic, coarsely chopped

4 stalks celery, thickly sliced (retain the young leaves for garnish)

1 x 800 g can whole peeled tomatoes, undrained

3 tablespoons tomato paste

6 sprigs thyme or 1 teaspoon dried thyme

6 sprigs oregano or 1 teaspoon dried oregano

salt and freshly ground black pepper

1/2 cup capers

10 pitted black olives

4 continental sausages, sliced

1. Boil 3 litres of salted water, add the fettucine and stir till the water returns to the boil. Let boil, uncovered, until the pasta is cooked and 'al dente'.

2. Drain, toss a little oil through the pasta and keep warm.

3. Meanwhile, heat the olive oil over a moderate heat in a large heavy-based pan. Cook the onions and garlic for 3 minutes, stirring, then add the celery, undrained tomatoes, tomato paste, herbs, and seasonings, and simmer gently for 15 minutes.

4. Add the capers, olives and sliced sausages and simmer for a further 5 minutes.

5. Toss the sauce through the pasta and serve immediately, garnished with the small, young celery leaves.

Serves 4–6 ◦ Preparation time: 5 minutes ◦ Cooking time: 25 minutes

Ⓖ LOW   OMEGA-3 *

| kJ/cal 1953/467 | PROTEIN 19g | FAT 12g | CARBOHYDRATE 69g | FIBRE 8g |

Tofu Chicken with Snow Peas and Hokkien Noodles, page 182

Chargrilled Vegetables and Beans with Pasta

2 small finger eggplants (approx. 160 g each), cut in half lengthwise

2 large red capsicum (approx. 350 g), seeded and cut into thick strips

6 Roma tomatoes (approx. 300 g), cut in half lengthwise

1 Spanish (red) onion (approx. 150 g), thickly sliced

4 cloves garlic, coarsely chopped

1 tablespoon olive oil

salt and freshly ground black pepper

1 x 400 g can borlotti beans, drained

250 g spirali pasta

½ bunch basil leaves, torn

1. Prepare the vegetables.

2. Brush the hotplate on the BBQ, or a large chargrill hotplate on the stovetop, with the olive oil, heat well and add all the prepared vegetables. Grind salt and pepper over the mixture and cook till the vegetables are golden brown, turning occasionally. Add the borlotti beans and toss through.

3. Meanwhile, boil 3 litres of salted water and cook the spirali, uncovered, for approx. 10 minutes or till 'al dente'. Drain.

4. On a large platter, heap the pasta and vegetables up, and scatter with torn basil leaves. Serve hot.

Serves 4 ◾ Preparation time: 15 minutes ◾ Cooking time: 15 minutes

Garlic Prawns, Red Capsicum and Coriander Pasta, page 179

 **LOW**   OMEGA-3 ˙

| kJ/cal **1533/366** | PROTEIN **14g** | FAT **7g** | CARBOHYDRATE **62g** | FIBRE **11g** |

Spaghetti with Steamed Greens

500 g wholemeal (or regular) spaghetti

4 large zucchini (approx. 150 g each)

12 snow peas, strings removed

50 g baby spinach leaves

1 tablespoon lemon juice

2 tablespoons olive oil

1 clove garlic, crushed

salt and freshly ground black pepper

8 basil leaves, torn

1 tablespoon sesame oil

2 tablespoons toasted sesame seeds

1. Boil the spaghetti in plenty of lightly salted water for 13 minutes or till tender. Drain and keep warm.

2. Meanwhile, top and tail the zucchini, and slice thinly lengthwise into long matchsticks. Wash and string the snow peas. Steam both till just softened and still bright green.

3. Mix together the lemon juice, olive oil, garlic and seasonings. Toss the vegetables, dressing, spinach and basil leaves through the spaghetti. Drizzle with sesame oil and sprinkle with toasted sesame seeds. Serve hot.

Serves 4–6 ▪ Preparation time: 5 minutes ▪ Cooking time: 13 minutes

NOTE: To toast raw sesame seeds, simply add to the dry, heated wok and toss continually till they begin to turn a light golden brown. Remove immediately to prevent burning, and cool.

Ⓖ **LOW**   OMEGA-3 *

| kJ/cal **1597/380** | PROTEIN **13g** | FAT **13g** | CARBOHYDRATE **53g** | FIBRE **15g** |

Garlic Prawns, Red Capsicum and Coriander Pasta

250 g spinach fettucine

500 g green king prawns, shelled and de-veined

4 cloves garlic, finely sliced

¼ cup (60 ml) extra virgin olive oil

salt and freshly ground black pepper

2 red capsicum (approx. 350 g), seeded and thinly sliced

½ bunch fresh coriander, coarsely chopped

1. Bring a large saucepan of salted water to the boil, add the pasta and cook for 11 minutes. Drain and toss in 1 tsp of olive oil.

2. Preheat the hot plate on the BBQ to moderately high.

3. Meanwhile, shell and de-vein the prawns, leaving heads and tails on. Toss with the sliced garlic and olive oil in a large bowl, and marinate for 10 minutes.

4. Tip the prawns, garlic and oil onto the hot BBQ and sear for 2 minutes.

5. Grind salt and freshly ground black pepper over the prawns.

6. On a large serving platter combine the drained pasta, prawns, capsicum strips and chopped coriander.

7. Serve hot with crusty low GI bread.

Serves 4–6 ⁄ Preparation time: 8 minutes ⁄ Cooking time: 11 minutes

 **LOW**   OMEGA-3 ⋯

kJ/cal 1367/326	PROTEIN 23g	FAT 11g	CARBOHYDRATE 33g	FIBRE 3g

Spiral Noodles with Smoked Chicken and Pinenuts

250 g spiral noodles

1 teaspoon salt

2 tablespoons pine nuts

2 small chillies, seeded and finely sliced

250 g smoked chicken breast (from a chicken shop or deli)

½ bunch flat leafed parsley, finely chopped

DRESSING

4 tablespoons olive oil

4 tablespoons balsamic vinegar

1 clove garlic, crushed

salt and freshly ground black pepper

1. Boil 4 litres of salted water and cook the noodles till tender. Refresh under cold running water.

2. Meanwhile, dry roast the pine nuts in a heavy-based frying pan, stirring constantly, till golden brown.

3. Finely slice the chillies and chicken breast.

4. Place all the dressing ingredients in a lidded jar and shake to combine.

5. Combine the noodles, pine nuts, chillies and chicken breast on a large platter, sprinkle with chopped parsley and pour the dressing over.

Serves 6 ⁄ Preparation time: 5 minutes ⁄ Cooking time: 10 minutes

Ⓖ **LOW** OMEGA-3 ·

| kJ/cal 1538/367 | PROTEIN 17g | FAT 20g | CARBOHYDRATE 30g | FIBRE 4g |

Marinated BBQ Chicken Noodle Salad

¼ teaspoon chilli flakes or 1 whole dried chilli, finely chopped

1 tablespoon canola oil

2 cloves garlic, finely chopped

2 strips lemon rind, finely chopped

500 g chicken thigh fillets, each sliced into 5 pieces

250 g spiral noodles

½ bunch fresh coriander, coarsely chopped

1. Combine the chilli, oil, garlic, lemon rind and chicken thigh fillet pieces in a bowl and marinate for 15 minutes.

2. Preheat the BBQ hotplate and cook the chicken pieces till golden brown, approx. 6 minutes.

3. Meanwhile, cook the spiral noodles in plenty of boiling, salted water for 10 minutes.

4. Drain and toss the chicken pieces and chopped coriander through the noodles, and serve immediately.

Serves 4 ⋅ Preparation time: 20 minutes ⋅ Cooking time: 10 minutes

Ⓖ **LOW** OMEGA-3 ⋯

| kJ/cal **1717/410** | PROTEIN **33g** | FAT **11g** | CARBOHYDRATE **44g** | FIBRE **3g** |

Tofu Chicken with Snow Peas and Hokkien Noodles

500 g chicken tenderloins, sliced into narrow strips

2 cloves garlic, finely chopped

1 tablespoon sesame oil

1/4 cup (60 ml) vegetable or chicken stock

300 g broccoli florets

80 g snow peas, strings removed

600 g fresh Hokkien noodles, soaked in boiling water

1 tablespoon toasted sesame seeds

MARINADE

3 tablespoons light soy sauce

1 tablespoon hoi sin sauce

1 tablespoon oyster sauce

1 tablespoon rice wine (mirin)

150 g firm tofu, diced

1. Combine the marinade ingredients in a large mixing bowl and toss the tofu cubes through the mixture.

2. Heat the sesame oil in a large wok and stir-fry the chicken and garlic for 3 minutes. Remove and set aside.

3. Add the stock and broccoli florets, cover and simmer for 3 minutes. Add the snow peas and cook a further minute.

4. Add the marinade and tofu, chicken and drained noodles. Toss to warm noodles. Serve hot, sprinkled with toasted sesame seeds.

Serves 6–8 ∎ Preparation time: 15 minutes ∎ Cooking time: 10 minutes

Ⓖ **LOW**   OMEGA-3 **

| kJ/cal **1400/530** | PROTEIN **24g** | FAT **8g** | CARBOHYDRATE **40g** | FIBRE **6g** |

Butter Bean, Capsicum and Prawn Pilaf

1 tablespoon canola oil

1 cup (200 g) Basmati rice

1 large brown onion (approx. 200 g), chopped

1 teaspoon turmeric

2 cloves garlic, chopped

1 large red capsicum (approx. 175 g), seeded and diced

1 x 400 g can whole peeled tomatoes, undrained

2 cups (500 ml) good chicken stock

salt and freshly ground black pepper

1 x 400 g can butter beans, drained

1 red chilli, seeded and finely sliced

500 g medium green prawns, shelled and de-veined

½ bunch fresh coriander, coarsely chopped

1. Heat the oil in a large, heavy-based frying pan and add the rice, onion and turmeric. Stir the rice for 3 minutes before adding the garlic, capsicum, tomatoes and juice, chicken stock and salt and pepper.

2. Cover the pan with a tight-fitting lid and simmer for 20 minutes, till most of the stock is absorbed by the rice.

3. Gently stir the butter beans, chilli and prawns through the mixture and cook, lidded, for a further 3 minutes.

4. Taste for seasoning, stir through the coriander and serve immediately.

Serves 4–6 ᴨ Preparation time: 10 minutes ᴨ Cooking time: 30 minutes

 **LOW**   OMEGA-3 ***

| kJ/cal **1200/280** | PROTEIN **24g** | FAT **4g** | CARBOHYDRATE **38g** | FIBRE **5g** |

Lime and Saffron Spatchcock on Bulgur

3 spatchcock (size 4)
½ teaspoon ground saffron or ground turmeric
1 tablespoon olive oil
2 cups (500 ml) chicken stock
1¾ cups (300 g) bulgur (cracked wheat)
flat leafed parsley for garnish

MARINADE
1 large red onion (approx. 200 g), finely chopped
5 tablespoons lime (or lemon) juice
salt and freshly ground black pepper

1. Preheat the oven to 190°C.

2. Wash out the cavities of the spatchcock with cold water and, using kitchen scissors, cut the spatchcock in half. Pat dry.

3. Mix the onion, lime juice, salt and pepper. Place each spatchcock half, cut side down, on a piece of foil, large enough to make a parcel, and cover the spatchcock with the marinade. Fold the foil up and place each parcel on a baking tray.

4. Mix the saffron with the oil in a small bowl.

5. Bake the spatchcock for 25 minutes, then open the foil and brush each piece with the saffron oil. Bake, uncovered, another 10 minutes.

6. Meanwhile, bring the stock to the boil. Place the bulgur in a heavy-based, lidded pan and pour the stock over. Cover and let simmer for 20 minutes or until all the liquid is absorbed.

7. Serve the spatchcock on a bed of hot bulgur, and garnish with flat leafed parsley. Accompany with a side dish of chargrilled vegetables.

Serves 6 ▪ Preparation time: 5 minutes ▪ Cooking time: 35 minutes

Ⓖ **LOW**   OMEGA-3 *

| kJ/cal 1365/326 | PROTEIN 32g | FAT 7g | CARBOHYDRATE 33g | FIBRE 9g |

Stuffed Eggplants

½ cup (100 g) pearl barley

3 cups (750 ml) water

2 medium sized eggplants (approx. 400 g each), halved lengthwise

2 ripe tomatoes (approx. 150 g each), finely diced

6 shallots, finely sliced

2 sprigs fresh oregano, or 1 teaspoon dried oregano

2 sprigs fresh marjoram, or 1 teaspoon dried marjoram

2 sprigs fresh thyme, or 1 teaspoon dried thyme

2 tablespoons olive oil

2 large cloves garlic, finely chopped

70 g parmesan cheese, grated

salt and freshly ground black pepper

few extra sprigs fresh oregano, marjoram or thyme for garnish

1. Preheat the oven to 180°C.

2. Simmer the pearl barley, covered, in the water for 30 minutes.

3. Meanwhile, scoop out the flesh of the eggplants, leaving a 1-cm shell. Sprinkle the shell with salt and turn upside down on kitchen paper to drain off the bitter juices. Dice the eggplant flesh.

4. Combine the diced tomatoes, sliced shallots and chopped herbs.

5. Heat the olive oil in a large, heavy-based frying pan and add the chopped garlic and diced eggplant. Sauté till the eggplant browns. Fold through the tomato mixture and drained barley, and stir in the parmesan cheese. Season with salt and freshly ground black pepper.

6. Rinse the eggplant shells out with cold water and pat dry. Fill with the stuffing and bake for 30 minutes.

7. Garnish with sprigs of fresh herbs and serve hot.

Serves 4 · Preparation time: 10 minutes · Cooking time: 40 minutes

 **LOW**   OMEGA-3 ·

| kJ/cal **1187/284** | PROTEIN **12g** | FAT **16g** | CARBOHYDRATE **22g** | FIBRE **8g** |

Roasted Sweet Potato, Garlic and Rosemary Pilaf

1 kg sweet potato, peeled and cubed

8 cloves garlic, peeled and halved

3 sprigs fresh rosemary

1 tablespoon olive oil

4 cups (1 litre) chicken stock, hot

1 tablespoon olive oil

2 cups (400 g) Basmati rice

salt and freshly ground black pepper

6 extra sprigs fresh rosemary

60 g freshly grated parmesan cheese

1. Preheat the oven to 200°C.

2. Place the cubed sweet potato, garlic cloves and sprigs of rosemary in a baking tray, and sprinkle with the olive oil.

3. Roast the sweet potato till just golden, approx. 20 minutes. Remove from the oven.

4. Heat the chicken stock to boiling point.

5. Heat the olive oil in a large, heavy-based, lidded saucepan and stir in the rice. Coat the rice with oil and cook for 2 minutes, stirring.

6. Add the sweet potato and garlic, and season with salt and pepper. Discard the rosemary sprigs. Add the hot chicken stock and turn the heat down to simmering.

7. Cover and cook gently for 15 minutes, till all the stock is absorbed and the rice is cooked through. Stir the parmesan through.

8. Turn the pilaf into 6 large pasta bowls, and decorate each with a fresh rosemary sprig.

Serves 6 ▪ Preparation time: 10 minutes ▪ Cooking time: 40 minutes

Ⓖ **MODERATE**   OMEGA-3 ▪

kJ/cal	**1894/452**	PROTEIN	**12g**	FAT	**10g**	CARBOHYDRATE	**78g**	FIBRE	**5g**

Chicken, Fennel and Lemon Paella

1 tablespoon olive oil
1 bulb fennel (approx. 400 g), finely sliced
1 small onion (approx. 100 g), finely sliced
2 cloves garlic, coarsely chopped
500 g chicken tenderloins, sinew removed
2 cups (400 g) Basmati rice
salt and freshly ground black pepper
4 cups (1 litre) chicken stock, boiling
1/2 bunch fresh dill, finely chopped (1/3 cup)
juice and zest of 1/2 lemon (50 ml)
60 g fresh parmesan cheese, shaved
a few sprigs of dill for decoration

1. Preheat the oven to 200°C.

2. Heat the oil in a large, ovenproof, heavy-based frying pan. Add the fennel, onion and garlic, and cook till they become opaque, approx. 2 minutes. Remove and set aside.

3. Add the tenderloins and cook for 3 to 4 minutes, till just cooked through. Remove and set aside.

4. Stir in the rice and cook for 2 minutes. Season.

5. Heat the chicken stock in a saucepan to boiling, then pour it into the frying pan. Stir the stock through the rice, and add the fennel, onion, garlic, chopped dill, and lemon juice and zest.

6. Place the pan in the oven and cook, uncovered, for 20 minutes.

7. Add the chicken tenderloins and parmesan and gently fork them through the rice.

8. Serve immediately, decorated with sprigs of dill.

Serves 6–8 ◾ Preparation time: 10 minutes ◾ Cooking time: 35 minutes

(G) **MODERATE**   OMEGA-3 ˙

kJ/cal 1351/323	PROTEIN 20g	FAT 8g	CARBOHYDRATE 43g	FIBRE 3g

Chapter 13

Mains and Accompaniments

Carrot and Thyme Tart

1 kg carrots, peeled and grated

1 large brown onion (approx. 200 g), peeled and grated

2 cloves garlic, grated or finely chopped

80 g low fat cheddar cheese, grated

⅓ cup (80 ml) canola oil

3 x 60 g omega-enriched eggs, lightly beaten

1 teaspoon ground nutmeg

salt and freshly ground pepper

1 tablespoon fresh thyme leaves, or 1 teaspoon dried

½ cup (75 g) wholemeal self-raising flour

1. Preheat the oven to 180°C.

2. Lightly oil a 30 cm round shallow quiche or pie dish.

3. Grate the carrots, onion, garlic and cheese (using the grating disc of your food processor makes this step quick and easy).

4. In a large mixing bowl beat together the oil, eggs, nutmeg, salt and pepper, and thyme leaves. Stir in the flour till combined, then add the carrots, onion, garlic and cheese.

5. Spoon into the prepared dish and bake for 45 minutes, till golden brown and cooked through.

Serves 6–8 ◾ Preparation time: 15 minutes ◾ Cooking time: 45 minutes

Ⓖ **LOW**   OMEGA-3 ***

kJ/cal 880/210	PROTEIN 8g	FAT 15g	CARBOHYDRATE 12g	FIBRE 6g

Pork Fillet with Spiced Pears and Basmati Rice

2 teaspoons olive oil

1 large brown onion (approx. 200g), cut into small dice

2 cloves garlic, finely chopped

2 sweet potato (approx. 250 g each), cut into small dice

1 cup (200 g) Basmati rice

1½ cups (375 ml) chicken stock

salt and freshly ground black pepper

4 Packham pears, peeled, cored and quartered

1 cinnamon stick

4 whole cloves

2 strips of lemon rind

¼ cup (50 g) raw sugar

1 teaspoon olive oil

1 clove garlic, finely chopped

500 g pork fillets

⅓ cup (80 ml) dry white wine

salt and freshly ground black pepper

½ bunch chives for garnish

1. Heat the oil in a large saucepan with a tight-fitting lid over a moderate heat. Add the onion, garlic and diced sweet potato and cook for 3 minutes, stirring.

2. Add the rice and cook for a further 3 minutes, stirring to coat the ingredients in oil and partially cook.

3. Pour in the chicken stock, season with salt and pepper, cover with a tight-fitting lid and turn the heat down to low. Simmer very gently for 15 minutes, till all the stock is absorbed and the rice cooked through.

4. Meanwhile, place the pears, cinnamon stick, cloves, lemon rind and sugar in a large saucepan and cover with 1 litre of water. Bring to the boil, then turn the heat down to gently simmer the pears, uncovered, for 20 minutes.

5. Heat the 1 teaspoon of oil in a heavy-based frying pan and brown the pork fillets on all sides. Continue to cook the fillets over a moderate heat for approx. 15 minutes, till just cooked through. Remove the fillets from the pan and rest them for 10 minutes in a warm place.

6. Add the garlic and white wine to the pan juices and simmer, stirring the sauce, for about 3 minutes. Season with salt and pepper.

7. Slice the pork fillets diagonally.

8. To assemble, place mounds of Basmati rice on warmed plates, top with slices of pork and pour the reduction sauce over the top. Garnish with whole chives. Fan the pear slices on the plate and pour a little juice over the top.

9. Serve hot, accompanied by steamed baby carrots.

Serves 4–6 ″ Preparation time: 10 minutes ″ Cooking time: 45 minutes

 LOW   OMEGA-3 *

kJ/cal **1534/366**   PROTEIN **24g**   FAT **3g**   CARBOHYDRATE **59g**   FIBRE **6g**

Roast Chicken with Apricot and Almond Stuffing

1 chicken (size 15/1.5 kg), skin and visible fat removed
½ cup (60 g) quick cook/instant barley
80 g dried apricots, coarsely chopped
50 g unblanched almonds, coarsely chopped
½ bunch flat leafed parsley, coarsely chopped
juice and zest of ½ lemon
1 x 60 g omega-enriched egg, lightly beaten
salt and freshly ground black pepper
1 tablespoon olive oil
2 cups (500 ml) chicken (or vegetable) stock

1. Preheat the oven to 180°C.

2. In a bowl, combine the uncooked barley, chopped apricots, almonds and parsley, juice and zest of lemon, lightly beaten egg, and season with salt and pepper.

3. Stuff the chicken and place, breast side up, in a lightly oiled baking dish. Tie the legs together with string and rub the chicken with the remaining olive oil. Pour the chicken stock into the dish.

4. Cover the dish with foil and place in the oven. Bake for one hour, then remove the foil and bake a further 30 minutes, basting the chicken with the stock to brown it up and keep it moist.

5. Remove the chicken from the dish and discard the string. Keep the chicken warm while making the sauce.

6. Make a reduction sauce by simmering the stock in the baking dish over a moderate heat to reduce by half. Season with salt and pepper and strain. Serve hot.

Serves 6 ▪ Preparation time: 10 minutes ▪ Cooking time: 1½ hours

Ⓖ **LOW**   OMEGA-3 ⋯

| kJ/cal 1527/365 | PROTEIN 40g | FAT 16g | CARBOHYDRATE 16g | FIBRE 4g |

Mediterranean Lasagne, page 201

Thai Green Chicken Curry

1 kg chicken breasts or thigh fillets, sliced thinly, fat removed

2 large onions (approx. 200 g), finely chopped

1 tablespoon canola oil

2 tablespoons green curry paste

1 stalk lemongrass

1½ cups (375 ml) chicken stock

200 ml low fat (lite) coconut milk

200 ml water

2 green chillies, finely sliced

250 g green beans, diagonally sliced

1 bunch fresh coriander, coarsely chopped

2 cups (400 g) Basmati rice

6 litres water

1. Heat the oil in a large heavy-based frying pan and add the onions. Cook gently for 5 minutes, then add the curry paste and cook for 2 minutes, stirring.

2. Crush the lemongrass stalk and add to the pan. Add the chicken stock, coconut milk and water and simmer for 10 minutes to reduce the liquid.

3. Add chillies and chicken. Simmer gently till the chicken is tender.

4. Bring the water to the boil and slowly pour the rice in, stirring till the water returns to the boil. Boil for 11 minutes, then drain immediately. Steam the green beans separately until just tender.

5. Remove the lemongrass from the curry, then finish adding the beans and chopped coriander.

6. Serve on a bed of hot Basmati rice with a garnish of coriander.

Serves 6–8 ▪ Preparation time: 5 minutes ▪ Cooking time: 17 minutes

ⓖ MODERATE   OMEGA-3 **

| kJ/cal 1680/401 | PROTEIN 33g | FAT 11g | CARBOHYDRATE 43g | FIBRE 4g |

Rack of Lamb with Lemon and Rosemary on Mash, page 196

Red Capsicum with Chargrilled Vegetables and Prawns

4 medium sized red capsicum (approx. 180 g each)

8 finger eggplants (approx. 80 g each)

12 small Roma tomatoes (approx. 80 g each)

2 tablespoons olive oil

4 cloves garlic, finely chopped

salt and freshly ground black pepper

2 bunches fresh basil

1 cup (90 g) penne pasta

150 g unblanched whole almonds, coarsely chopped

4 cloves garlic, peeled

¼ cup (60 ml) extra virgin olive oil

salt and freshly ground black pepper

16 green king prawns, shelled and de-veined, leaving the tail on

1. Preheat the oven to 180°C and the chargrill to hot.

2. Halve the capsicum from the stalk down. Remove the seeds and white membrane from the inside cavities. Halve the eggplants lengthwise, leaving the stalks on. Halve the Roma tomatoes lengthwise.

3. Combine the olive oil, chopped garlic, salt and freshly ground black pepper. Use half the mixture to brush the tomatoes and top with ½ bunch of basil leaves, shredded. Place on an oven tray and bake for 30 minutes in the preheated oven.

4. Place the capsicum halves, cut side down, on a baking tray and bake in the oven till they soften but do not lose shape. Remove and pat dry with paper kitchen towel.

5. Boil 4 litres of salted water and cook the penne for 14 minutes, till tender. Drain and toss with a little olive oil.

6. Brush the halved eggplant and the prawns with the remaining garlic and olive oil mixture, and chargrill till tender (approx. 3 minutes).

7. Make a pesto with the remaining basil leaves. First use a food processor to process the almonds coarsely. Add the garlic, olive oil, salt and freshly ground black pepper and remaining basil leaves, and process to a coarse puree.

8. To assemble, fill the capsicum shells with the roasted tomatoes and baked basil leaves, pasta, eggplant halves, and chargrilled prawns. Top with a large dollop of pesto.

Serves 8 ▪ Preparation time: 20 minutes ▪ Cooking time: 30 mins

Ⓖ LOW   OMEGA-3 **

| kJ/cal 986/236 | PROTEIN 13g | FAT 13g | CARBOHYDRATE 17g | FIBRE 6g |

Rack of Lamb with Lemon and Rosemary on Mash

2 racks of lamb, 6 chops each
3 cloves garlic
6 sprigs fresh rosemary
zest of 1 lemon
freshly ground black pepper
2 tablespoons olive oil
6 sprigs fresh rosemary for garnish
Sweet Potato, Potato and Garlic Mash (page 205)

1. Preheat the oven to 200°C.

2. Trim the racks of lamb with a small knife to remove all visible fat and to neaten them up. Peel and halve the cloves of garlic, and break the rosemary sprigs into smaller sprigs. Remove the zest from the lemon with a zester or vegetable peeler.

3. Cut a tunnel between the bone and the meat, and fill with garlic halves, lemon zest and a couple of rosemary sprigs.

4. Pierce the lamb and insert sprigs of rosemary over the surface of the rack.

5. Place the racks in a baking dish, grind a little black pepper over them and sprinkle with olive oil.

6. Bake for 35 to 40 minutes in the preheated oven until cooked through but slightly pink.

7. Let the lamb rest for 5 minutes in a warm place before cutting into cutlets.

8. Serve on a bed of hot Sweet Potato, Potato and Garlic Mash. Decorate with a sprig of fresh rosemary.

Serves 6 ∎ Preparation time: 10 minutes ∎ Cooking time: 40 minutes

(G) **ZERO**   OMEGA-3 *

| kJ/cal 743/178 | PROTEIN 17g | FAT 12g | CARBOHYDRATE neg | FIBRE neg |

Chargrilled Blue Eye Cod with Warm Borlotti Bean Salad

2 x 400 g cans borlotti beans, ½ cup liquid reserved

1 cup (250 ml) chicken stock

3 cloves garlic, crushed

2 large ripe tomatoes (approx. 200 g), coarsely chopped

2 bunches rocket lettuce, washed and coarsely chopped

1 bunch shallots, finely sliced

¼ bunch flat leafed parsley, finely chopped

3 tablespoons lemon juice

1 tablespoon olive oil

4 x 120 g blue eye cod cutlets

freshly ground black pepper

extra rocket lettuce leaves for garnish

1. In a bowl, mash ½ cup of borlotti beans with a little reserved liquid from the can.

2. Place the mashed beans, remaining whole beans, chicken stock, garlic, tomatoes, chopped rocket lettuce, sliced shallots, chopped parsley, lemon juice, salt and pepper in a large saucepan.

3. Warm the bean mixture, covered, over a low heat for approx. 10 minutes, while cooking the cod.

4. Preheat the BBQ chargrill or chargrill plate on the stove and brush with olive oil. Grind black pepper over the cod cutlets and cook for approximately 8 minutes, turning once only.

5. Serve the warm bean salad as a bed for the blue eye cod cutlets, and garnish with extra rocket lettuce leaves.

Serves 4 ▪ Preparation time: 10 minutes ▪ Cooking time: 8 minutes

 LOW   OMEGA-3 ****

| kJ/cal 1192/285 | PROTEIN 32g | FAT 10g | CARBOHYDRATE 17g | FIBRE 10g |

Deep Sea Perch on Roasted Vegetables

6 x 150 g deep sea perch fillets

1 tablespoon olive oil

3 medium zucchini (approx. 100 g each), thickly sliced

6 ripe tomatoes (approx. 1 kg), quartered

2 red onions (approx. 400 g), cut into wedges

1 large red capsicum (approx. 200 g), thickly sliced

1 large green capsicum (approx. 200 g), thickly sliced

4 large cloves garlic, coarsely chopped

8 sprigs fresh thyme or 2 tablespoons dried thyme leaves

2 tablespoons olive oil

salt and freshly ground black pepper

½ bunch fresh basil, leaves finely sliced

3 tablespoons balsamic vinegar

1. Preheat the oven to 250°C

2. Season the deep sea perch fillets with freshly ground black pepper, and brush with a little olive oil.

3. In a large baking dish, combine the prepared vegetables, garlic, thyme and olive oil, and spread in one layer. Grind salt and pepper over the vegetables.

4. Bake the vegetables in the preheated oven for 20 minutes. Arrange the fillets over the vegetables and roast for 7 to 10 minutes.

5. Transfer the fillets carefully to a warm plate and cover.

6. Arrange the vegetables on 6 warm plates and sprinkle with the basil leaves and a drizzle of balsamic vinegar. Top with the fillets and serve immediately with Basmati rice.

Serves 6 ▪ Preparation time: 15 minutes ▪ Cooking time: 30 minutes

(G) **ZERO**   OMEGA-3 ****

| kJ/cal **999/239** | PROTEIN **29g** | FAT **10g** | CARBOHYDRATE **7g** | FIBRE **5g** |

Seared Tuna with Red Capsicum Sauce

1 tablespoon olive oil
6 tuna steaks (approx. 1 kg)
4 cloves garlic, peeled and halved
salt and freshly ground black pepper
juice and zest of 1 lemon
1½ cups (300 g) Basmati rice
SAUCE
4 large, very red capsicums (approx. 800 g)
1 x 800 g can whole peeled tomatoes, drained
salt and freshly ground black pepper

1. Preheat a large, heavy-based frying pan, or the BBQ hotplate, and brush the tuna steaks with oil. Add a little oil to the pan or hotplate and heat the garlic through.

2. Add the tuna steaks, searing each side, then leave them, without turning, for 6 to 8 minutes, till just cooked through. Remove the tuna and garlic from the pan and discard the garlic.

3. If using a pan, heat the pan juices with lemon juice and season with salt and pepper. Pour the sauce over the tuna steaks. Pour boiling water over the lemon zest to use as garnish. Drain and set aside.

4. Bring a large pot of salted water to the boil and cook the Basmati rice for 11 minutes. Drain in a colander and keep warm.

5. To make the sauce, halve and seed the capsicums and grill, skin side up, till black and blistered. Place in a paper bag and let cool before removing the skin. Puree with tomatoes in a food processor. Season with salt and pepper and warm through.

6. Serve tuna on a bed of Basmati rice. Garnish with the lemon zest. Spoon the sauce around the plate and serve immediately.

Serves 6 ◾ Preparation time: 10 minutes ◾ Cooking time: 35 minutes

Ⓖ **MODERATE**   OMEGA-3 *****

| kJ/cal **1835/438** | PROTEIN **42g** | FAT **9g** | CARBOHYDRATE **48g** | FIBRE **5g** |

Deep Sea Bream Fillets with Semi-dried Tomato Marinade

1 cup (170 g) semi-dried tomatoes in oil (reserve the oil)
2 cloves garlic, peeled and coarsely chopped
juice and zest of 1 lemon
freshly ground black pepper
1 kg deep sea bream fillets
flat leafed parsley for garnish

1. Place the drained semi-dried tomatoes, $^1/_4$ cup of the reserved oil, garlic cloves, lemon juice, zest and pepper in the food processor, and blend to a smooth consistency.

2. Place the sea bream fillets in a shallow casserole dish, spread the marinade over, cover with foil and marinate for 30 minutes.

3. Preheat the oven to 180°C.

4. Bake the fillets, covered, till just cooked through, approx. 15 minutes. Remove from the oven and serve on a bed of steamed Basmati rice, with the marinade spooned over the top. Decorate with a few sprigs of flat leafed parsley.

Serves 6 ª Preparation time: 35 minutes ª Cooking time: 15 minutes

Ⓖ **MODERATE**   OMEGA-3 ****

kJ/cal 1250/300	PROTEIN 37g	FAT 12g	CARBOHYDRATE 11g	FIBRE 3g

Mediterranean Lasagne

1 tablespoon olive oil

500 g premium beef mince

2 brown onions (approx. 300 g), chopped

4 cloves garlic, chopped

1 x 800 g tin whole peeled tomatoes

½ cup (50 g) tomato paste

1 cup (250 ml) water

½ bunch fresh oregano, chopped

2 eggplants (approx. 500 g), cut into ½-cm slices

1 tablespoon olive oil

1 x 250 g packet frozen chopped leaf spinach, thawed

1 teaspoon nutmeg

5 sheets large instant lasagne pasta

100 g low fat cheddar cheese, grated

salt and freshly ground black pepper

1. Preheat the oven to 180°C.

2. Heat the oil in a large heavy-based saucepan over moderate heat. Add the onions and garlic and cook, stirring occasionally, for 3 minutes.

3. Add the mince and cook till the meat turns brown, then add the tomatoes, tomato paste and water. Season with salt and pepper and add the chopped oregano. Cook for 30 minutes, stirring occasionally.

4. Brush the eggplant slices with oil and grill till browned on each side.

5. Using a rectangular casserole dish, approx. 23 cm x 34 cm, layer the ingredients. Start with half the meat sauce, then 2½ sheets of lasagne, half the eggplant slices, all the spinach sprinkled with nutmeg, salt and pepper, 2½ sheets lasagne pasta, eggplant slices, meat sauce and grated cheese.

6. Bake for 40–45 minutes. Serve with a crisp green salad.

Serves 6–8 ▪ Preparation time: 15 minutes ▪ Cooking time: 75 minutes

Ⓖ **LOW**   OMEGA-3 *

kJ/cal 1189/284	PROTEIN 23g	FAT 11g	CARBOHYDRATE 24g	FIBRE 6g

Seared Atlantic Salmon Fillets with White Bean Puree

4 Atlantic salmon fillets (200 g each), trimmed and boned
1 tablespoon olive oil
2 cloves garlic, halved

WHITE BEAN PUREE
1 x 400 g can cannellini beans, drained
2 cloves garlic, crushed
1½ tablespoons lemon juice
4 sprigs fresh thyme leaves or 1 tablespoon dried thyme
2 teaspoons olive oil
salt and freshly ground black pepper
1 bunch rocket lettuce leaves

1. Preheat the hotplate of the BBQ or a heavy-based frying pan.

2. Using a food processor (or mash by hand), process the drained beans, garlic, lemon juice, thyme leaves, olive oil, salt and pepper to a smooth, soft puree. Place in an ovenproof or microwave bowl, cover and warm through in a low oven or microwave.

3. To cook the Atlantic salmon fillets, heat the oil with the garlic cloves for 1 minute on the hotplate. Add the salmon fillets and cook for approximately 5 to 8 minutes, turning once only.

4. Place a large spoonful of cannellini bean puree in the centre of heated plates, arrange rocket leaves on top, and finish with the cooked fillets.

5. Drizzle a little extra oil around the plate and serve immediately.

Serves 4 ▪ Preparation time: 10 minutes ▪ Cooking time: 5–8 minutes

Ⓖ **LOW**   OMEGA-3 *****

kJ/cal 1389/332	PROTEIN 46g	FAT 13g	CARBOHYDRATE 7g	FIBRE 5g

Chargrilled Garlic Potatoes and Sweet Potatoes

1 kg waxy potatoes, e.g. pontiac or desiree

1 kg sweet potatoes

6 cloves garlic, coarsely chopped

1 sprig fresh rosemary or 1 tablespoon dried rosemary

1/3 cup (80 ml) extra virgin olive oil

salt and freshly ground black pepper

a few extra sprigs rosemary for garnish

1. Peel the potatoes and sweet potatoes, and parboil in plenty of boiling salted water. Drain and set aside.

2. Preheat a lightly oiled chargrill or large heavy-based frying pan.

3. Mix the chopped garlic, rosemary, oil and seasonings together in a large mixing bowl. Cut the vegetables into large chunks and toss in the garlic oil.

4. Cook on the hot chargrill or frying pan till golden brown and crisp.

5. Serve hot in a large bowl with sprigs of fresh rosemary for garnish.

Serves 6–8 ₪ Preparation time: 10 minutes ₪ Cooking time: 20 minutes

Ⓖ MODERATE

| kJ/cal 1039/248 | PROTEIN 6g | FAT 10g | CARBOHYDRATE 34g | FIBRE 4g |

Chickpea, Tomato and Eggplant

1 x 400 g can chickpeas, drained

6 finger eggplants (approx. 100 g each)

2 large onions, (approx. 200 g each)

4 cloves garlic, peeled

2 tablespoons olive oil

$\frac{1}{2}$ teaspoon ground cumin

$\frac{1}{2}$ teaspoon ground cinnamon

$\frac{1}{2}$ teaspoon ground coriander

salt and freshly ground black pepper

2 x 800 g cans whole peeled tomatoes, undrained

1. Drain the chickpeas, rinse well and set aside.

2. Dice the eggplants and onions, and finely chop the garlic.

3. Heat the olive oil in a large heavy-based frying pan, and gently cook the eggplants, onions, garlic and spices over a moderate heat for 10 minutes, stirring occasionally.

4. Season with salt and pepper, and add the undrained tomatoes, breaking them up with a wooden spoon. Add the drained chickpeas, cover and simmer for 20 minutes.

5. Serve warm with low GI crusty bread as an entrée, or as a side dish to the main course.

Serves 8 as entrée, 6 as side dish ≈ Preparation time: 5 minutes ≈ Cooking time: 30 minutes

Ⓖ **LOW**

| kJ/cal 539/129 | PROTEIN 5g | FAT 6g | CARBOHYDRATE 14g | FIBRE 6g |

Sweet Potato, Potato and Garlic Mash

5 sweet potatoes (approx. 750 g)
2 potatoes (approx. 150 g each)
2 whole cloves garlic
1 tablespoon olive oil
2 sprigs fresh oregano, chopped, or 1 tablespoon dried oregano
salt and freshly ground black pepper

1. Peel and cut the sweet potatoes and potatoes into chunks. Place in hot water in a large saucepan and add the garlic cloves.

2. Cook in plenty of salted boiling water till tender, about 20 minutes.

3. Drain and reserve $^1/_2$ cup of the cooking water. Mash the drained sweet potato, potato and garlic with olive oil, chopped oregano and seasonings with a little reserved cooking water to moisten.

Serves 8 ▪ Preparation time: 10 minutes ▪ Cooking time: 20 minutes

Ⓖ **MODERATE**

| kJ/cal **800/191** | PROTEIN **5g** | FAT **5g** | CARBOHYDRATE **32g** | FIBRE **4g** |

Chapter 14

Desserts

Poached Pears with Rich Chocolate Sauce

6 medium sized pears (approx. 200 g each),
peeled, cored and quartered
1½ litres water
1 cup (200 g) raw sugar
1 cinnamon stick
juice and rind of 1 lemon

CHOCOLATE SAUCE
130 g dark chocolate, chopped into small pieces
1 tablespoon canola oil
25 ml cold water

1. Heat the water, sugar, cinnamon stick, juice and lemon rind in a large saucepan, and simmer for 5 minutes. Add the pear slices and simmer for 20 minutes, uncovered. Cool.

2. Make the sauce by placing all the ingredients in a small saucepan. Heat gently, stirring occasionally. When combined, pour over the pears. Serve immediately with a dollop of low fat plain yoghurt.

Serves 6 ▪ Preparation ime: 10 minutes ▪ Cooking time: 20 minutes

Ⓖ **LOW**   OMEGA-3 *

kJ/cal 1250/300	PROTEIN 2g	FAT 10g	CARBOHYDRATE 55g	FIBRE 5g

Poached Peaches in Lemongrass Syrup

2 cups (500 ml) dry white wine
2 cups (500 ml) water
1 stalk lemongrass, finely sliced
1 x 2 cm piece fresh ginger, finely sliced
1 bayleaf
½ cup (120 g) raw sugar
6 large slipstone peaches (approx. 300 g each), halved

1. Simmer the wine, water, lemongrass, ginger, bayleaf and raw sugar in a large saucepan for 5 minutes.

2. Add the halved peaches and poach for a further 5 minutes. Remove the peach halves with a slotted spoon and peel away their skins. Simmer the syrup to reduce by half and strain.

3. Serve peach halves with a dollop of low fat plain yoghurt, and a drizzle of syrup.

Serves 6 ∥ Preparation time: 2 minutes ∥ Cooking time: 10 minutes

Ⓖ **LOW**

| kJ/cal **669/160** | PROTEIN **2g** | FAT **neg** | CARBOHYDRATE **25g** | FIBRE **2g** |

Poached Peaches in Lemongrass Syrup, this page

Bread and Butter Pudding

2½ cups (600 ml) low fat milk

4 x 60 g omega-enriched eggs

½ cup (120 g) caster sugar

2 teaspoons vanilla essence

2–3 slices raisin bread, crusts removed (e.g. Bürgen™ Mixed Grain Fruit Loaf)

2 teaspoons canola margarine

1. Preheat the oven to 160°C. Lightly butter a 6-cup (1½ litre) ovenproof dish.

2. Pour the milk into the dish and add the eggs, sugar and vanilla. Whisk together till combined.

3. Lightly butter the raisin bread and cut each slice diagonally. Arrange, butter side up, on top of the milk.

4. Bake for 1 hour, till the bread puffs up and turns golden brown.

Serves 4 ▫ Preparation time: 5 minutes ▫ Cooking time: 1 hour

Lemon Semolina Puddings with Berry Coulis, page 210

Ⓖ **LOW**   OMEGA-3 ***

| kJ/cal **1523/364** | PROTEIN **18g** | FAT **9g** | CARBOHYDRATE **56g** | FIBRE **2g** |

Lemon Semolina Puddings with Berry Coulis

2 cups (600 ml) low fat milk

½ cup (100 g) fine semolina

¼ cup (60 g) sugar

1 teaspoon vanilla essence

zest of 1 large lemon

1 x 60 g omega-enriched egg, lightly beaten

300 g blackberries/strawberries/raspberries

2 tablespoons icing sugar

½ cup (125 ml) white wine or apple juice

1. Preheat the oven to 180°C. Lightly oil six ½-cup souffle dishes. Line the base of each dish with baking paper.

2. Pour the milk, semolina and sugar in a saucepan and bring to the boil, stirring constantly. Reduce the heat and stir for 1 more minute.

3. Remove from the heat and stir in the vanilla essence and lemon zest.

4. Cover the surface of the mixture with plastic wrap to prevent a skin forming, and cool. When cooled, stir in the beaten egg.

5. Spoon the mixture into the prepared dishes and place them into a baking pan with enough boiling water to reach halfway up the sides of the dishes. Cover loosely with a large sheet of foil. Carefully slide the pan into the oven and poach the puddings for 15 minutes, till set. Remove the puddings from the pan of water. Run a knife around the puddings, turn out onto serving plates and remove the piece of baking paper.

6. Meanwhile, puree most of the berries with the icing sugar. (Reserve some whole berries for decoration if desired). Thin the coulis with white wine or apple juice.

7. Pour the coulis around the puddings, and decorate with slivers of lemon peel or whole berries (optional).

Serves 6 ⁄ Preparation time: 10 minutes ⁄ Cooking time: 15 minutes

 LOW   OMEGA-3 *

| kJ/cal 814/195 | PROTEIN 8g | FAT 3g | CARBOHYDRATE 35g | FIBRE 2g |

Individual Apple and Ginger Crumbles

6 (approx. 1 kg) Granny Smith apples, peeled, cored and sliced

1 cup (250 ml) water

2 tablespoons raw sugar

1 cinnamon stick

3 cloves

3 tablespoons glacé ginger, coarsely chopped (optional)

CRUMBLE

½ cup (80 g) self-raising flour

2 tablespoons margarine

¼ cup (60 g) dark brown sugar, tightly packed

½ cup (60 g) rolled barley

½ teaspoon ground nutmeg

1. Preheat the oven to 180°C. Set out six 1-cup capacity souffle dishes.

2. Place the prepared apples, water, sugar, cinnamon stick and cloves in a medium sized saucepan and simmer for 15 minutes, till the apples are just cooked. Remove the cinnamon stick and cloves, and mix 2 tablespoons of the glacé ginger through the apples.

3. Meanwhile, place the flour in a mixing bowl and rub the margarine through. Mix in the brown sugar, barley and nutmeg.

4. Fill the souffle dishes with the apples and ginger, and top with the crumble mixture.

5. Bake for 30 minutes and remove from the oven. Decorate each crumble with the remaining tablespoon of chopped ginger, and serve hot with a dollop of low-fat vanilla yoghurt.

Serves 6 ⁎ Preparation time: 10 minutes ⁎ Cooking time: 45 minutes

Ⓖ LOW   OMEGA-3 *

| kJ/cal 1089/260 | PROTEIN 3g | FAT 6g | CARBOHYDRATE 50g | FIBRE 4g |

Summer Pudding

300 g fresh or frozen raspberries/blackberries/mulberries
(a few reserved for decoration)
¼ cup (60 g) raw sugar
¼ cup (125 ml) red wine
¼ cup (125 ml) water
1 cinnamon stick
8 slices Performax™ day-old bread, crusts removed

1. Combine most of the berries, sugar, red wine, water and cinnamon stick in a medium sized saucepan and gently simmer for 5 minutes, till the berries are plump and slightly softened. Discard the cinnamon stick and cool.

2. Line a 475-ml soup bowl or mould with 6 slices of bread, cut into triangles, and overlapping so they form a casing for the berries when the pudding is turned out. Cut the remaining two slices to cover the top of the bowl.

3. Spoon a little of the berry juice over the slices to moisten them, and with a slotted spoon, fill the bowl with the berries. Pour ¼ cup of the berry juice over the berries and top with the remaining bread to make a lid. Reserve any remaining berry juice.

4. Cover with a sheet of plastic wrap, place a plate on top and weigh down with a weight. Place in the refrigerator overnight.

5. Turn out onto a white plate, decorate with reserved berries and any reserved juice, and serve with a dollop of low fat yoghurt.

Serves 4 ⫽ Preparation time: 10 minutes ⫽ Cooking time: 5 minutes

 MODERATE

| kJ/cal 1022/243 | PROTEIN 9g | FAT 2g | CARBOHYDRATE 49g | FIBRE 7g |

PART FOUR

the
Life Plan
tables

TABLES OF GLYCEMIC INDEX (GI) AND GLYCEMIC LOAD (GL)

* indicates that the food has so little carbohydrate that the GI cannot be tested. The GL is therefore 0.

FOOD	GI GLUCOSE =100	NOMINAL SERVE SIZE (G)	AVAIL. CARB IN SERVE (G)	GL PER SERVE
All-Bran™, breakfast cereal	30	30	15	4
All-Bran Fruit 'n Oats™, breakfast cereal	39	30	17	7
All-Bran Soy 'n Fibre™, breakfast cereal	33	30	14	4
Angel food cake, 1 slice	67	50	29	19
Apple, 1 medium	38 (av)	120	15	6
Apple, dried	29	60	34	10
Apple juice, pure, unsweetened, reconstituted	40	250ml	29	12
Apple muffin	44	60	29	13
Apple, oat and sultana muffin (from mix)	54	50	26	14
Apricots, fresh, 3 medium	57	120	9	5
Apricots, canned in light syrup	64	120	19	12
Apricots, dried	30	60	27	8
Apricot, coconut and honey muffin (from mix)	60	50	26	16
Arborio, risotto rice, boiled	69	150	53	36
Bagel, white	72	70	35	25
Baked beans, canned in tomato sauce	48 (av)	150	15	7
Banana, raw, 1 medium	52 (av)	120	24	12
Banana cake, 1 slice	47	80	38	18
Banana, oat and honey muffin (from mix)	65	50	26	17
Barley, pearled, boiled	25 (av)	150	42	11
Basmati, white, boiled, 1 cup	58	150	38	22
Beef	*	120	0	0
Beetroot, canned	64	80	7	5
Bengal gram dhal, chickpea	11	150	36	4
Black bean soup	64	250	27	17
Black beans, boiled	30	150	23	7
Blackbread, Riga	76	30	13	10
Blackeyed beans, soaked, boiled	42	150	30	13

FOOD	GI GLUCOSE =100	NOMINAL SERVE SIZE (G)	AVAIL. CARB IN SERVE (G)	GL PER SERVE
Blueberry muffin	59	57	29	17
Bran Flakes™, breakfast cereal	74	30	18	13
Bran muffin	60	57	24	15
Breakfast Bar, Fibre Plus™ bar	78	30	23	18
Breton wheat crackers	67	25	14	10
Broad beans	79	80	11	9
Broken rice, white, cooked in rice cooker	86	150	43	37
Buckwheat	54 (av)	150	30	16
Pancakes, buckwheat, gluten-free, made from packet mix	102	77	22	22
Bulgur, boiled 20 min	48 (av)	150	26	12
Bun, hamburger	61	30	15	9
Bürgen® Oat Bran & Honey Loaf with Barley	31	30	10	3
Bürgen® Soy-Lin, kibbled soy (8%) and linseed (8%) loaf	36	30	9	3
Bürgen® Fruit Loaf	44	30	13	6
Bürgen® Mixed Grain	49 (av)	30	11	6
Burger Rings™, barbeque-flavored	90	50	31	28
Butter beans, dried, cooked 1.25 h	31	150	20	6
Calrose, white, medium grain, boiled	83	150	43	36
Capellini pasta, boiled	45	180	45	20
Carrots, peeled, boiled	49	80	5	2
Cheese	*	120	0	0
Cherries, raw	22	120	12	3
Chickpeas, canned in brine	42	150	22	9
Chickpeas, dried, boiled	28 (av)	150	30	8
Chicken nuggets, frozen, reheated in microwave oven 5 min	46	100	16	7
Chocolate, milk	42	50	31	13
Chocolate, white, Milky Bar®	44	50	29	13

FOOD	GI GLUCOSE =100	NOMINAL SERVE SIZE (G)	AVAIL. CARB IN SERVE (G)	GL PER SERVE
Chocolate butterscotch muffins, made from packet mix	53	50	28	15
Chocolate cake made from packet mix with chocolate frosting	38	111	52	20
Chocolate mousse, 2% fat	31	50	11	3
Chocolate pudding, made from powder and whole milk	47	100	16	7
Coca Cola®, soft drink	53	250	26	14
Coco Pops™	77	30	26	20
Condensed milk, sweetened	61	250	136	83
Cordial, orange, reconstituted	66	250	20	13
Corn chips, plain, salted	42	50	25	11
Cornflakes™, breakfast cereal	77	30	25	20
Cornflakes Crunchy Nut™, breakfast cereal	72	30	24	17
Cornmeal, boiled in salted water 2 min	68	150	13	9
Corn pasta, gluten-free	78	180	42	32
Corn Pops™, breakfast cereal	80	30	26	21
Corn Thins, puffed corn cakes, gluten-free	87	25	20	18
Couscous, boiled 5 min	65 (av)	150	35	23
Cranberry juice cocktail	52	250	31	16
Crispix™, breakfast cereal	87	30	25	22
Croissant	67	57	26	17
Crumpet	69	50	19	13
Crunchy Nut Cornflakes™ bar	72	30	26	19
Crunchy Nut™ Cornflakes	72	30	24	17
Cupcake, strawberry-iced	73	38	26	19
Custard, home made from milk, wheat starch, and sugar	43	100	17	7
Custard, prepared from powder with whole milk, no bake	35	100	17	6

FOOD	GI GLUCOSE =100	NOMINAL SERVE SIZE (G)	AVAIL. CARB IN SERVE (G)	GL PER SERVE
Custard, TRIM™, reduced-fat	37	100	15	6
Custard apple, raw, flesh only	54	120	19	10
Dark rye, Blackbread, Riga	76	30	13	10
Dark rye, Schinkenbrot, Riga	86	30	14	12
Dates, dried	103	60	40	42
Desiree potato, peeled, boiled 35 min	101	150	17	17
Dietworks Hazelnut & Apricot bar	42	50	22	9
Digestives plain, 2 biscuits	59 (av)	25	16	10
Doongara, rice, white	56 (av)	150	39	22
Egg Custard, prepared from powder with whole milk, no bake	35	100	17	6
Eggs	*	120	0	0
English Muffin™ bread	77	30	14	11
Ensure™, vanilla drink	48	250mL	34	16
Ensure™ bar, chocolate fudge brownie	43	38	20	8
Ensure Plus™, vanilla drink	40	237mL	47	19
Ensure Pudding™, old fashioned vanilla	36	113	26	9
Fanta®, orange soft drink	68	250	34	23
Fettucine, egg, cooked	32	180	46	15
Figs, dried, tenderised	61	60	26	16
Fish	*	120	0	0
Fish Fingers	38	100	19	7
Flan cake	65	70	48	31
French Baguette, white, plain	95	30	15	15
French fries, frozen, reheated in microwave	75	150	29	22
French vanilla cake made from packet mix with vanilla frosting	42	111	58	24
French vanilla ice-cream, premium, 16% fat	38	50	9	3
Froot Loops™, breakfast cereal	69	30	26	18

FOOD	GI GLUCOSE =100	NOMINAL SERVE SIZE (G)	AVAIL. CARB IN SERVE (G)	GL PER SERVE
Frosties™, sugar-coated Cornflakes	55	30	26	15
Fructose, pure	19 (av)	10	10	2
Fruit cocktail, canned	55	120	16	9
Fruit Fingers, Heinz Kidz™, banana	61	30	20	12
Fruit loaf, Bürgen™	44	30	13	6
Fruit Loaf, dense continental style wheat bread with dried fruit	47	30	15	7
Fruit and Spice Loaf, thick sliced	54	30	15	8
Gatorade® sports drink	78	250	15	12
Glucodin™ glucose tablets	102	50	50	50
Gluten-free white bread, sliced	80	30	15	12
Gluten-free multigrain bread	79	30	13	10
Muesli, gluten-free with 1.5% fat milk	39	30	19	7
Gluten-free corn pasta	78	180	42	32
Gluten-free rice and maize pasta	76	180	49	37
Gluten-free split pea and soya pasta shells	29	180	31	9
Gluten-free spaghetti, rice and split pea, canned in tomato sauce	68	220	27	19
Glutinous rice, white, cooked in rice cooker	92 (av)	150	48	44
Gnocchi	68	180	48	33
Golden Wheats™, breakfast cereal	71	30	23	16
Grapefruit, raw	25	120	11	3
Grapefruit juice, unsweetened	48	250	20	9
Grapes, green	46 (av)	120	18	8
Green pea soup, canned	66	250	41	27
Guardian™	37	30	12	5
Hamburger bun	61	30	15	9
Haricot/Navy beans	38 (av)	150	31	12
Healthwise™ breakfast cereal for bowel health	66	30	18	12

FOOD	GI GLUCOSE =100	NOMINAL SERVE SIZE (G)	AVAIL. CARB IN SERVE (G)	GL PER SERVE
Healthwise™ breakfast cereal for heart health	48	30	19	9
Helga's™ Classic Seed Loaf	68	30	14	9
Helga's™ traditional wholemeal bread	70	30	13	9
Honey	55 (av)	25	18	10
Honey & Oat bread, Vogel's	55	30	14	7
Honey Rice Bubbles™, breakfast cereal	77	30	27	20
Honey Smacks™, breakfast cereal	71	30	23	11
Ice-cream, regular fat	61 (av)	50	13	8
Ice-cream, low fat, vanilla, 'Light'	50	50	6	3
Ice-cream, premium, French vanilla, 16% fat	38	50	9	3
Ice-cream, premium, Ultra chocolate, 15% fat	37	50	9	4
Instant potato, prepared	85 (av)	150	20	17
Instant rice, white, cooked 6 min	87	150	42	36
Ironman PR bar®, chocolate	39	65	26	10
Isostar® sports drink	70	250	18	13
Jam, Apricot fruit spread, reduced sugar	55	30	13	7
Jam, strawberry	51	30	20	10
Jasmine rice, white, cooked in rice cooker	109	150	42	46
Jatz™, plain salted cracker biscuits	55	25	17	10
Jelly Beans	78 (av)	30	28	22
Jevity™, fibre enriched drink	48	237mL	36	17
Just Right™, breakfast cereal	60	30	22	13
Just Right Just Grains™, breakfast cereal	62	30	23	14
Kaiser rolls	73	30	16	12
Kavli™ Norwegian Crispbread	71	25	16	12
Kidney beans, canned	52	150	17	9
Kidz™, Heinz, Fruit Fingers, banana	61	30	20	12
Kidney beans, boiled	28 (av)	150	25	7

FOOD	GI GLUCOSE =100	NOMINAL SERVE SIZE (G)	AVAIL. CARB IN SERVE (G)	GL PER SERVE
Kiwi fruit	58	120	12	7
Komplete™, breakfast cereal	48	30	21	10
K-Time Just Right™ breakfast cereal bar	72	30	24	17
K-Time Strawberry Crunch™ breakfast cereal bar	77	30	25	19
Kudos Whole Grain Bars, chocolate chip	62	50	32	20
Lactose, pure	46 (av)	10	10	5
Lamb	*	120	0	0
Lamingtons, sponge dipped in chocolate and coconut	87	50	29	25
L.E.A.N Fibergy™ bar, Harvest Oat	45	50	29	13
L.E.A.N Life long Nutribar™, Peanut Crunch	30	40	19	6
L.E.A.N Life long Nutribar™, Chocolate Crunch	32	40	19	6
L.E.A.N Nutrimeal™, drink powder, Dutch Chocolate	26	250	13	3
Lebanese bread, white, 1 round	75	30	16	12
Lentil, canned	44	250	21	9
Lentils, green, boiled	30 (av)	150	17	5
Lentils	29 (av)	150	18	5
Lentils, red, boiled	26	150	18	5
Life Savers®, peppermint candy	70	30	30	21
Light rye	68	30	14	10
Lima beans, baby, frozen, reheated in microwave oven	32	150	30	10
Linguine pasta, thick, cooked	46	180	48	22
Linguine pasta, thin, cooked	52	180	45	23
Linseed rye	55	30	13	7
Lucozade®, original sparkling glucose drink	95	250	42	40

FOOD	GI GLUCOSE =100	NOMINAL SERVE SIZE (G)	AVAIL. CARB IN SERVE (G)	GL PER SERVE
Lungkow beanthread noodles	26	180	45	12
Lychee, canned in syrup, drained	79	120	20	16
M & M's®, peanut	33	30	17	6
Macaroni, cooked	47 (av)	180	48	23
Macaroni and Cheese, boxed	64	180	51	32
Maltose, 50 g	105	10	10	11
Mango (Mangifera indica)	51	120	15	8
Marmalade, orange (Australia)	48	30	20	9
Mars Bar®	62	60	40	25
Melba toast, Old London	70	30	23	16
Milk, full-fat cow's milk, fresh	31	250ml	12	4
Milk, skim	32	250	13	4
Milk, low fat, chocolate, with sugar, Lite White™	34	250	26	9
Milk, condensed, sweetened	61	50	136	83
Milk Arrowroot™ biscuits	69	25	18	12
Milky Bar®, Chocolate, white	44	50	29	13
Millet, boiled	71	150	36	25
Milo™, chocolate powder, dissolved in water	55	250	16	9
Mini Wheats™, whole wheat breakfast cereal	58	30	21	12
Mini Wheats™, blackcurrant whole wheat breakfast cereal	72	30	21	15
Mixed grain loaf, Bürgen®	49 (av)	30	11	6
Morning Coffee™, 3 biscuits	79	25	19	15
Mousse, butterscotch, 1.9% fat	36	50	10	4
Mousse, chocolate, 2% fat	31	50	11	3
Mousse, hazelnut, 2.4% fat	36	50	10	4
Mousse, mango, 1.8% fat	33	50	11	4
Mousse, mixed berry, 2.2% fat	36	50	10	4

FOOD	GI GLUCOSE =100	NOMINAL SERVE SIZE (G)	AVAIL. CARB IN SERVE (G)	GL PER SERVE
Mousse, strawberry, 2.3% fat	32	50	10	3
Muesli bar containing dried fruit	61	30	21	13
Muesli, gluten-free with 1.5% fat milk	39	30	19	7
Muesli, toasted	43	30	17	7
Muesli, Swiss Formula	56	30	16	9
Multi-Grain 9-Grain	43	30	14	6
Mung bean noodles (Longkou beanthread), dried, boiled	39	180	45	18
Nesquik™, chocolate dissolved in 1.5% fat milk	41	250	11	5
Nesquik™, strawberry dissolved in 1.5% fat milk	35	250	12	4
New Potato, unpeeled and boiled 20 min	78	150	21	16
New Potato, canned, heated in microwave 3 min	65	150	18	12
No Bake Egg Custard, prepared from powder with whole milk	35	100	17	6
Noodles, Instant 'two-minute' Maggi®	46	180	40	19
Noodles, mung bean (Longkou beanthread), dried, boiled	39	180	45	18
Noodles, rice, freshly made, boiled	40	180	39	15
Nutella®, chocolate hazelnut spread	33	20	12	4
Nutrigrain™, breakfast cereal	66	30	15	10
Oat 'n Honey Bake™, breakfast cereal	77	30	17	13
Oat Bran & Honey Loaf with Barley, Bürgen®	31	30	10	3
Oat bran, raw	55 (av)	10	5	3
Oatmeal™, Highland biscuits	55	25	18	10
Orange, 1 medium	42 (av)	120	11	5
Orange cordial, reconstituted	66	250	20	13
Orange juice, unsweetened, reconstituted	53	250ml	18	9

FOOD	GI GLUCOSE =100	NOMINAL SERVE SIZE (G)	AVAIL. CARB IN SERVE (G)	GL PER SERVE
Pancakes, prepared from shake mix	67	80	58	39
Pancakes, buckwheat, gluten-free, made from packet mix	102	77	22	22
Parsnips	97	80	12	12
Party pies, beef	45	100	27	12
Pastry	59	57	26	15
Paw paw (Carica papaya)	56	120	8	5
Peach, fresh, 1 large	42 (av)	120	11	5
Peach, canned in heavy syrup	58	120	15	9
Peach, canned in light syrup	52	120	18	9
Peach, canned in reduced-sugar syrup, SPC Lite	62	120	17	11
Peanuts, roasted, salted	14 (av)	50	6	1
Pear, raw	38 (av)	120	11	4
Pear halves, canned in natural juice	43	120	13	5
Pear halves, canned in reduced-sugar syrup, SPC Lite	25	120	14	4
Peas, dried, boiled	22	150	9	2
Peas, green, frozen, boiled	48 (av)	80	7	3
Pelde brown rice, boiled	76	150	38	29
Performax™ Country Life Bakery	38	30	13	5
Pikelets, Golden brand	85	40	21	18
Pineapple, raw	66	120	10	6
Pineapple juice, unsweetened	46	250	34	15
Pinto beans, canned in brine	45	150	22	10
Pinto beans, dried, boiled	39	150	26	10
Pita bread, white	57	30	17	10
Pizza, cheese	60	100	27	16
Pizza, Super Supreme, pan (11.4% fat)	36	100	24	9
Pizza, Super Supreme, thin and crispy (13.2 % fat)	30	100	22	7

FOOD	GI GLUCOSE =100	NOMINAL SERVE SIZE (G)	AVAIL. CARB IN SERVE (G)	GL PER SERVE
Ploughman's™ Wholegrain, original recipe	47	30	14	7
Ploughman's™ Wholemeal, smooth milled (Quality Bakers, Australia)	64	30	13	9
Plums, raw	39	120	12	5
Pontiac, peeled, boiled 35 min	88	150	18	16
Pontiac, peeled and microwave on high for 6-7.5 min	79	150	18	14
Pontiac, peeled, cubed, boiled 15 min, mashed	91	150	20	18
Pop Tarts™, Double Chocolate	70	50	36	25
Popcorn, plain, cooked in microwave oven	72	20	11	8
Pork	*	120	0	0
Porridge	42	250	21	9
Potato, baked	85 (av)	150	30	26
Potato crisps, plain, salted	57	50	18	10
Pound cake	54	53	28	15
Power Bar®, chocolate	56 (av)	65	42	24
Premium Soda Crackers	74	25	17	12
Pretzels, oven-baked, traditional wheat flavour	83	30	20	16
Prunes, pitted, 6	29	60	33	10
Pudding, instant, chocolate, made from powder and whole milk	47	100	16	7
Pudding, instant, vanilla, made from powder and whole milk	40	100	16	6
Pudding, Sustagen™, Instant vanilla, made from powdered mix	27	250	47	13
Puffed Crispbread	81	25	19	15
Puffed rice cakes, white	82	25	21	17
Puffed Wheat, breakfast cereal	80	30	21	17
Pumpernickel rye kernel bread	41	30	12	5

FOOD	GI GLUCOSE =100	NOMINAL SERVE SIZE (G)	AVAIL. CARB IN SERVE (G)	GL PER SERVE
Pumpkin	75	80	4	3
Quik™, chocolate (Nestlé, Australia), dissolved in 1.5% fat milk	41	250	11	5
Quik™, strawberry (Nestlé, Australia), dissolved in 1.5% fat milk	35	250	12	4
Raisins	64	60	44	28
Ravioli, durum wheat flour, meat filled, boiled	39	180	38	15
Real Fruit Bars, strawberry processed fruit bars	90	30	26	23
Real Fruit Bars, strawberry processed fruit bars	90	30	26	23
Rice and maize pasta, Ris'O'Mais, gluten-free	76	180	49	37
Rice Bran, extruded	19	30	14	3
Rice Bubbles™, breakfast cereal	87	30	26	22
Rice Bubble Treat™ bar	63	30	24	15
Rice cakes, white	82	25	21	17
Rice Krispies™, breakfast cereal	82	30	26	22
Rice noodles, freshly made, boiled	40	180	39	15
Rice pasta, brown, boiled 16 min	92	180	38	35
Rice vermicelli, Kongmoon	58	180	39	22
Rich Tea, 2 biscuits	55	25	19	10
Risotto rice, Arborio, boiled	69	150	53	36
Rockmelon/Cantaloupe, raw	65	120	6	4
Roggenbrot, Vogel's	59	30	14	8
Roll (bread), Kaiser	73	30	16	12
Rolled oats	42	250	21	9
Roll-Ups®, processed fruit snack	99	30	25	24
Romano beans	46	150	18	8
Rye bread	58 (av)	30	14	8

FOOD	GI GLUCOSE =100	NOMINAL SERVE SIZE (G)	AVAIL. CARB IN SERVE (G)	GL PER SERVE
Ryvita™ crackers	69	25	16	11
Salami	*	120	0	0
Sao™, plain square crackers	70	25	17	12
Sausages, fried	28	100	3	1
Scones, plain, made from packet mix	92	25	9	7
Sebago potato, peeled, boiled 35 min	87	150	17	14
Semolina *(Triticum aestivum)*, steamed	55	67 (dry)	50	28
Shellfish (prawns, crab, lobster etc)	*	120	0	0
Shortbread biscuits	64	25	16	10
Shredded Wheat, breakfast cereal	75 (av)	30	20	15
Shredded Wheatmeal™ biscuits	62	25	18	11
Skittles®	70	50	45	32
Snickers Bar®	41	60	36	15
So Natural™ soy milk, full-fat (3%), 120 mg calcium, Calciforte	36	250	18	6
So Natural™ soy milk, reduced-fat (1.5%), 120 mg calcium, Light	44	250	17	8
So Natural™ soy milk, full-fat (3%), 0 mg calcium, Original	44	250	17	8
So Natural™ soy smoothie drink, banana, 1% fat	30	250	22	7
So Natural™ soy smoothie drink, chocolate hazelnut, 1% fat	34	250	25	8
So Natural™ soy yoghurt, peach and mango, 2% fat, sugar	50	200	26	13
Soda Crackers, Premium	74	25	17	12
Soft drink, Coca Cola®	53	250	26	14
Soft drink, Fanta®, orange	68	250	34	23
Sourdough rye	48	30	12	6
Sourdough wheat	54	30	14	8

FOOD	GI GLUCOSE =100	NOMINAL SERVE SIZE (G)	AVAIL. CARB IN SERVE (G)	GL PER SERVE
Soy milk, So Natural™ full-fat (3%), 120 mg calcium, Calciforte	36	250	18	6
Soy milk, So Natural™ reduced-fat (1.5%), 120 mg calcium, Light	44	250	17	8
Soy milk, So Natural™ full-fat (3%), 0 mg calcium, Original	44	250	17	8
Soy smoothie drink, So Natural™ banana, 1% fat	30	250	22	7
Soy smoothie drink, So Natural™ chocolate hazelnut, 1% fat	34	250	25	8
Soy yoghurt, So Natural™ peach and mango, 2% fat, sugar	50	200	26	13
Soya beans, dried, boiled	20	150	6	1
Soya beans, canned	14	150	6	1
Soy-Lin, Bürgen® kibbled soy (8%) and linseed (8%) loaf	36	30	9	3
Spaghetti, gluten-free, rice and split pea, canned in tomato sauce	68	220	27	19
Spaghetti, white, boiled 5 minutes	38 (av)	180	48	18
Spaghetti, wholemeal, boiled 5 minutes	37	180	42	16
Special K™, breakfast cereal	54	30	21	11
Spirali, durum wheat, white, boiled to al denté texture	43	180	44	19
Split pea and soya pasta shells, gluten-free	29	180	31	9
Split Pea soup	60	250	27	16
Split peas, yellow, boiled 20 min	32	150	19	6
Sponge cake, plain	46	63	36	17
Sports Plus®, sport drink	74	250	17	13
Star Pastina, white, boiled 5 minutes	38	180	48	18
Stoned Wheat Thins	67	25	17	12
Strawberry jam	51	30	20	10

FOOD	GI GLUCOSE =100	NOMINAL SERVE SIZE (G)	AVAIL. CARB IN SERVE (G)	GL PER SERVE
Stuffing, bread	74	30	21	16
Sucrose	68 (av)	10	10	7
Sultana Bran™, breakfast cereal	73	30	19	14
Sultanas	56	60	45	25
Sunbrown Quick™ rice, boiled	80	150	38	31
Sunflower and barley bread, Riga	57	30	11	6
Super Supreme pizza, pan (11.4% fat)	36	100	24	9
Super Supreme pizza, thin and crispy (13.2 % fat)	30	100	22	7
Sushi, salmon	48	100	36	17
Sustagen™ Hospital with extra fiber, drink made from powdered mix	33	250mL	44	15
Sustagen™ milk, Dutch Chocolate	31	250mL	41	13
Sustagen™ pudding, Instant vanilla, made from powdered mix	27	250	47	13
Sustagen Sport®, sport drink	43	250	49	21
Sustain™, breakfast cereal	68	30	22	15
Sustain™ cereal bar	57	30	25	14
Swede (rutabaga)	72	150	10	7
Sweet corn, whole kernel, canned, diet-pack, drained	46	150	28	13
Sweet potato, Ipomoea batatas	44	150	25	11
Sweetened condensed milk	61	250	136	83
Taco shells, cornmeal-based, baked	68	20	12	8
Tapioca boiled with milk	81	250	18	14
Tapioca (Manihot Utilissima), steamed 1 h	70	250	18	12
Team™, breakfast cereal	82	30	22	17
Tofu-based frozen dessert, chocolate with high-fructose (24%) corn syrup (USA)	115	50	9	10
Tomato soup	38	250	17	6
Tortellini, cheese	50	180	21	10

FOOD	GI GLUCOSE =100	NOMINAL SERVE SIZE (G)	AVAIL. CARB IN SERVE (G)	GL PER SERVE
Total™, breakfast cereal	76	30	22	17
TRIM™ custard, reduced-fat	37	100	15	6
Tuna	*	120	0	0
Twisties™, cheese-flavoured, extruded snack, rice and corn	74	50	29	22
Twix® Cookie Bar, caramel	44	60	39	17
Ultra chocolate ice-cream, premium 15% fat	37	50	9	4
Vaalia™, reduced-fat apricot & mango yoghurt	26	200	30	8
Vaalia™, reduced-fat French vanilla yoghurt	26	200	10	3
Vaalia™, diet, mango yoghurt, sweetened with acesulfame K and Splenda	23	200	14	3
Vaalia™, diet, mixed berry yoghurt, sweetened with acesulfame K and Splenda	25	200	13	3
Vaalia™, diet, strawberry yoghurt, sweetened with acesulfame K and Splenda	23	200	13	3
Vaalia™, diet, vanilla yoghurt, sweetened with acesulfame K and Splenda	23	200	13	3
Vaalia™, reduced-fat tropical passionfruit yoghurt drink	38	200	29	11
Vanilla cake made from packet mix with vanilla frosting	42	111	58	24
Vanilla pudding, instant, made from powder and whole milk	40	100	16	6
Vanilla Wafers, 6 biscuits	77	25	18	14
Veal	*	120	0	0
Vermicelli, white, boiled	35	180	44	16

FOOD	GI GLUCOSE =100	NOMINAL SERVE SIZE (G)	AVAIL. CARB IN SERVE (G)	GL PER SERVE
Vita-Brits™, breakfast cereal	68	30	20	13
Vitari, wild berry, non-dairy, frozen				
fruit dessert	59	100	21	12
Vogel's Honey & Oats	55	30	14	7
Vogel's Roggenbrot	59	30	14	8
Waffles	76	35	13	10
Water crackers	78	25	18	14
Watermelon, raw	72	120	6	4
Weis Mango Frutia™, low fat frozen				
fruit dessert	42	100	23	10
Weet-Bix™, breakfast cereal	69	30	17	12
Wheat-bites™, breakfast cereal	72	30	25	18
White bread, wheat flour	70	30	14	10
Wholemeal bread, wheat flour	77	30	12	9
Wonderwhite™ bread	80	30	14	11
Yam, peeled, boiled	37 (av)	150	36	13
Yoghurt drink Vaalia™, reduced-fat				
tropical passionfruit	38	200	29	11
Yoghurt, low fat, fruit with artificial				
sweetener	14	200	13	2
Yoghurt, low fat, fruit with sugar	33	200	31	10
Yoghurt, low fat (0.9%), wild strawberry	31	200	30	9

Glossary

amino acids These are the building blocks of protein. There are more than 20 different types of amino acids in foods, and our body uses these to assemble its own proteins.

antioxidant Any substance that inhibits oxidation of another substance. Oxidation is a natural process that occurs in the body all the time, but it is implicated specifically in the development of disease processes such as cardiovascular disease, cancer and ageing. Dietary antioxidants are believed to limit these disease processes.

atherogenic Contributing to the development of atheroma, a build-up of fatty and fibrous material in the walls of arteries. This causes the arteries to thicken, harden and become less elastic. In the blood vessels of the heart this contributes to heart disease or atherosclerosis.

bioavailable This refers to the degree to which a substance is available to the body to use once consumed.

etiology The study of the causes of disease.

flavonoids A sub-group of polyphenols (phytochemicals) that has antioxidant abilities.

glycogen The form in which carbohydrate is stored in muscles and the liver.

haem iron The form of iron found in red meat, liver, seafood and poultry. It is absorbed more easily than non-haem iron.

HDL cholesterol High-density lipoprotein cholesterol, also known as 'good' cholesterol because elevated levels of it protect against heart disease.

homocysteine A substance normally produced in the body in metabolising the amino acid methionine. Elevated levels are associated with an increased risk of blood vessel disease.

insulinemia The presence of insulin in the blood.

isoflavones A type of phytoestrogen particularly found in soybeans.

LDL cholesterol Low-density lipoprotein cholesterol, also known as 'bad' cholesterol because elevated levels of it are a risk factor for heart disease.

lignans Phytoestrogens found in cereal grains and seeds; for example, linseeds.

lipids Another term for fats.

omega-3 fats Certain polyunsaturated fats that are essential in our diet because our body cannot make them. They are required for normal growth and development and play a beneficial role in infant brain and eye development, rheumatoid arthritis, heart disease, diabetes and cancer.

omega-3 equivalents Certain fatty acids that can be converted into long chain omega-3 fatty acids by the body. Alpha-linolenic acid is an example.

lycopene An antioxidant found in tomatoes, tomato products and watermelon. It is known to protect against prostate cancer.

macronutrients The major nutrients required by the body, including protein, fat, carbohydrate and water.

metabolism The process by which the body uses nutrients to yield energy and dissipate waste products.

micronutrients Nutrients present in food and required by the body in relatively small amounts, including vitamins and minerals.

nitrosamines Potentially carcinogenic substances formed from amines and nitrites in foods.

non-haem iron The form of iron found in breads, fruit, vegetables, cereals, legumes, nuts and eggs. It is less well absorbed by the body than haem iron.

phytochemicals Natural chemicals, found in all plant foods, which can produce an array of health benefits.

phytoestrogens Plant chemicals that are similar in structure to the oestrogens produced in our body and having similar, although weaker, effects. Examples include isoflavones in soy and lignans in linseeds.

polyphenols A group of phytochemicals found in fruits, grains, vegetables, wine, tea, cocoa and chocolate, which is believed to have antioxidant properties.

trans-fatty acids A cholesterol-raising form of fat found in dairy foods, some meats, butter and some margarines.

triglycerides The chemical name for fats stored and circulated in our body. A triglyceride consists of three fatty acids attached to one glycerol molecule.Index

Index

Aboriginal diets 7, 36, 89
acacia seeds 7
American Diabetes Association
    63, 67
amylopectin 19, 78
amylose 19, 78
archeological record 28
arteriosclerosis 46
arthritis 31, 45
Asian-style diets 73–83
asthma 45
auto-immune diseases 31
avocados 26, 97

baisen 29
balsamic vinegar 128
barley 109
basmati rice 78, 80
beancurd 76–77
beans 22, 76, 77, 113, 115
beef 124
biscuits 23, 110
blood pressure 44, 59–60
blood sugar levels 7, 9, 11–12,
    17–29
Boyd Eaton, Dr S. 86–88, 90
brain development 31, 45
breads 23, 28, 29, 107–111
breast cancer 76
breast milk 45
bulgur 109
butter 40

calcium 39
cancer
    avoiding 75
    breast 45, 76
    colon 45
    rates in other countries 57,
        58, 73
    reduced risk of 31
canned fish 47, 52–54, 120
canola oil 34, 40, 125, 127
carbohydrates 7, 8, 11, 17–29,
    62–64, 88, 155
'Carbohydrates in Health, Expert
    Report on' 25
cardiovascular disease. see heart
    disease

carotenoids 74
cereals 22, 23, 28, 29, 107–111
chapati 29
cheeky yam 7
cheeses 39
cholesterol 35, 59, 123
cod liver oil 120
Colagiuri, Dr Stephen 7
cold pressed oils 127
copha 40
Cordain, Professor Loren 13, 87
corn 109–110
corn oil 40
coronary disease. see heart
    disease
Crete 58

dairy products 39, 51–52, 90
DASH (Dietary Approaches to
    Stop Hypertension) 60
depression 31, 36
diabetes 7, 8, 11, 26–27, 62–64,
    73, 132
diets
    Aboriginal 7, 36, 89
    Asian-style 73–83
    Greek 57
    Inuit (Eskimo) 74
    Japanese 58
    Mediterranean-style 11–12,
        34, 57–71
    varieties of 90
    vegetarian 86
doongara rice 80

eggs 50, 123–124
Eskimo (Inuit) diets 74
exercise 131–133

fats
    concealed 33
    food labels and 35
    heart disease and 26–27
    low fat diets 11–12
    necessity of, in diet 31
    omega-3 and -6 37–38, 43–55
    in recipes 154–155
    saturated 31–32, 40–41, 125,
        126
    solid and liquid 36–37
    sugar–fat seesaw 24
    trans-fatty acids 32–34, 38
fibre 88, 155
fish 43, 45, 47, 52–54, 118–121
Flatt, Jean-Pierre 64
flaxseed oil 40

flour 29
folate 59
Food and Agriculture
    Organisation 25
food labels 35
food processing 19, 28
free fatty acids 64–65
fruits 22, 23, 74, 99, 106

genetic make-up 85–86
ghee 40
G.I. Factor, The (book) 7, 8, 25,
    60, 78
glucose. see glycaemic index
    (G.I.)
Glucose Revolution, The. see
    The G.I. Factor
glutinous rice 78
glycaemic index (G.I.)
    blood sugar levels 18
    carbohydrates 17
    factors influencing 21
    history of 7–10
    measurement of 20
    obesity and 27, 29
    publications about 25–27
    rating 155
    sport and 27, 29
    starch and 19
    substituting foods 23
    symbol 10
glycerol 38
grains 13, 22–23, 28–29, 73, 78,
    80–81, 107–111
Greek diets 57
greens 102

Harvard University studies 25
heart disease
    Asian-style diets and 73
    coronary 11–12
    fats and 31
    glycaemic index and 25–27,
        29
    Mediterranean-style diets and
        57–60
    omega-3 fats and 43–44
    omega-6 fats and 46
    soy and 76
    walking and 133
hypertension 44, 59–60

insulin levels 11–12, 18, 65–66,
    90
intelligence 31
Inuit (Eskimo) diets 74

Japanese diets 58

kidney beans 115
kidney problems 62
lamb 124
Lancet, The 25–26
learning ability 31
Lee, Dr Richard, Man the Hunter 87
legumes 22
lentils 113, 115
linseed oil 40, 127
Lyon Heart Study 34, 57, 59

maize 109–110
mammoths 89–90
margarine 32, 34
meats 26, 32, 52, 75, 89–90, 123–124
Mediterranean-style diets 11–12, 34, 57–71
metabolic evolution 85–86
milk 22, 45, 51
minerals 89
monounsaturated products 126. see also fats
MUFA (monounsaturated fatty acids) 60–69
multivitamin supplements 74
mustard seed oil 41, 125, 127

New York Times 25
noodles 80–81, 112
nuts 26, 55, 97, 117

oats 110
obesity 11, 27, 29, 57, 73
offal 74
oils
    necessity of, in diet 31
    polyunsaturated fat content 48–49
    recommended 32, 40, 41, 120, 125
    saturated 40–41
    vegetable 37
olive oil 34, 40, 41, 97, 125, 127–128

omega-3 and omega-6 fatty acids
    chemistry of 37–38
    content in foods 48–55
    coronary heart disease and 46
    effect on health 45
    in oils/fats 40–41, 120, 125
    prehistoric ratios of 90
    rating 154
    ratios of 46
overconsumption 57, 66
overweight 11, 27, 29, 57, 73

paleolithic nutrition 85–93
palm oil 41
pancreas 18
pasta 58, 80–81, 112
peanut oil 41
peas 22, 113, 115
phytochemicals 77
P:M:S ratio 37
polyunsaturated. see also fats
    fats 48–55
    products 126
porridge 110
potatoes 23
pregnancy 45
processed foods 19, 28
proteins 12–13, 62–63, 85–93, 155
psoriasis 45
pulses 113, 114
pumpernickel 29

red wine 97
renal failure 62
rheumatoid arthritis 45
rice 23, 73, 78, 80–81, 110
rice wine vinegar 128
rye 111

salad 99
salad dressings 50
saturated fats 31–32, 40–41, 125, 126. see also fats
seafoods 36, 118–121
seaweed 73

seeds 55
shellfish 47
sourdough breads 29
soybean oil 41
soybeans 73, 76, 77
spaghetti 21
spinach 102–103
split peas 115
sport 27, 29
spreads 48–49
sprouted wheat breads 29
starch 19
sticky rice 78
stone ground flour 29
sugar 24
Sunola™ 40, 41
supplements (multivitamin) 74
sweet potato 103
sweetcorn 109–110
Sydney University Glycaemic Index Research Service (SUGiRS) 10

tofu 76–77
tomatoes 104
trans-fatty acids 32, 34, 36–41
triglycerides 11, 38

vegetable oils 37
vegetables 22, 26, 74, 99, 100–101
vegetarian diets 86
vinegar 97, 128
vitamins
    paleolithic 89
    supplements 74

walking 131–133
websites 10, 25
weight 11, 57, 64–66, 73
wheat 111
wheat breads 29
wholegrain breads 28, 107
wine (red) 97
wine vinegar 128
World Health Organisation 25

yam, cheeky 7

Recipe Index

Apple and ginger crumbles 212
Apricot and muesli muffins 159
Atlantic salmon fillets, seared, with white
  bean puree 202

Baby pea and ham soup 163
Baby spinach salad 102
Beans
  butter bean, capsicum and prawn
    pilaf 183
  cannelini 115
  garbanzo 115
  green bean, rocket, baby tomato and
    olive salad 172
  red kidney 115
  warm borlotti bean sala with chargrilled
    blue eye cod 197
Beef
  chilli 124
  Mediterranean casserole 124
Biscuits, oat 110
Blue eye cod, chargrilled, with warm
borlotti
  bean salad 197
Bread and butter pudding 209
Bream fillets, deep sea, with semi-dried
  tomato marinade 200
Burgers, chickpea 116
Butter bean, capsicum and prawn pilaf
  183

Capsicum, corn and barley patties 157
Capsicum, red, with chargrilled
  vegetables and prawns 94-195
Carrot and thyme tart 189
Celery, walnut and lemon thyme salad
  171
Chick nuts 117

Chicken
  avocado, sprout and ricotta bake 162
  chunky vegetable and pasta soup 168
  fennel, and lemon paella 187
  lime and saffron spatchcock on bulgur
    184
  marinated BBQ, and noodle salad 181
  roast, with apricot and almond stuffing
    192
  smoked, with spiral noodles and pine
    nuts 180
  Thai green chicken curry 193
  tofu, with snow peas and hokkien
    noodles 182
Chickpeas
  basic recipe 115
  burgers 116
  chick nuts 117
  curry 116
  dip 116
  salad, warm 116
  tomato and eggplant 204

Chilli beef 124
Choc chip muffins 160
Chocolate sauce 207
Cod, blue eye, chargrilled with warm
borlotti
  bean salad 197
Corn, capsicum and barley patties 157
Cornmeal, capsicum and chive muffins
  158
Croutons 128
Crumbles, individual apple and ginger 212
Curry
  chickpea 116
  Thai green chicken 193

Deep sea bream fillets with semi-dried
  tomato marinade 200
Deep sea perch on roasted vegetables
  198

Dip, chickpea 116
Dressing
    Asian-style 74
    honey-soy, with spinach 102
    Mediterranean-style 128

Eggplants, stuffed 185

Fennel chicken and lemon paella 187
Fettuccine with vegetables and sausage
    176
Fettuccine, fresh with scallops 175
Figs, grilled 106
Fish
    see also Tuna
    chargrilled blue eye cod with warm
        borlotti bean salad 197
    deep sea bream fillets with semi-dried
        tomato marinade 200
    deep sea perch on roasted vegetables
        198
    good grilled fish fillets 121
    salmon and butter bean salad 120
    sardine toast topper 120
    seared Atlantic salmon fillets with
        white bean puree 202
    with tomato and beans 121
Fruit, poached 106

Garlic prawns, red capsicum and
    coriander pasta 179
Green bean, rocket, baby tomato an
    olive salad 172
Grilled figs 106
Grilled red capsicum, sweet potato and
    herb salad 173

Hearty winter vegetable soup 165
Hokkien noodles with tofu chicken and
    snow peas 182
Hummus 116
Turkish 161

Lamb
    Mediterranean casserole 124
    rack of, with lemon and rosemary on
        mash 196
    salad, warm 124
Lasagne, Mediterranean 201
Lemon semolina puddings with berry
    coulis 210-211
Lentils 115
Lime and saffron spatchcock on bulgur
    184
Lunchtime tuna 121

Marinade
    for lamb 127
    marinated BBQ chicken noodle salad
        181
    semi-dried tomato, with deep sea
        bream fillets 200
Meatless Mediterranean roast103
Mediterranean casserole 124
Mediterranean lasagne 201
Mediterranean pasta sauce 112
Mediterranean style dressing 128
Muffins
    apricot and muesli 159
    choc chip 160
    cornmeal, capsicum and chive 158

Noodles
    hokkien, with tofu chicken and snow
        peas 182
    instant 112
    salad with marinated BBQ chicken 181
    spiral, with smoked chicken and pine
        nuts 180

Oat biscuits 110

Paella, lemon, and fennel chicken 187
Pasta
    chunky vegetable, chicken and pasta

soup 168
coriander, with garlic prawns and red
capsicum 179
fettuccine with vegetables and
sausage 176
fresh fettuccine with scallops 175
spaghetti with steamed greens 178
with chargrilled vegetables and beans
177
Patties, capsicum, corn and barley 157
Pea, baby, and ham soup 163
Peaches, poached in lemongrass syrup
208
Pears, poached with rich chocolate sauce
207
Perch, deep sea, on roasted vegetables
198
Pilaf
butter bean, capsicum and prawn 183
roasted sweet potato, garlic and
rosemary 186
Poached fruit 106
Poached peaches in lemongrass syrup
208
Poached pears with rich chocolate sauce
207
Pork fillet with spiced pears and basmati
rice 190-191
Potatoes, chargrilled garlic, and sweet
potatoes 203
Prawns with red capsicum and chargrilled
vegetables 194-195
Prawns, garlic, with red capsicum and
coriander pasta 179
Pudding
bread and butter 209
lemon semolina with berry coulis
210-211
summer 213
Pulses, dried (preparation) 114
Pumpkin, sweet potato and cumin dhal
soup 167

Rack of lamb with lemon and rosemary
on mash 196
Red capsicum with chargrilled vegetables
and prawns 194-195
Roast chicken with apricot and almond
stuffing 192
Roast chicken, garlic and borlotti bean
soup 166
Roast, meatless Mediterranean 103
Roasted sweet potato 103
Roasted sweet potato, garlic and
rosemary pilaf 186
Roasted tomatoes, slow 104
Roma tomato, mint and cucumber salad
170

Salad. see also Dressing
baby spinach 102
borlotti bean, warm, with chargrilled
blue eye cod 197
celery, walnut and lemon thyme 171
chickpea, warm 116
green bean, rocket, baby tomato and
olive 172
grilled red capsicum, sweet potato and
herb 173
lamb, warm 124
marinated BBQ chicken and noodle
181
roma tomato, mint and cucumber 170
salmon and butter bean 120
three bean and basil 169
Salmon and butter bean salad 120
Salmon fillets, seared Atlantic, with white
bean puree 202
Salsa, tomato 104
Sardine toast topper 120
Sauce
basic tomato 104
chocolate 207
Mediterranean pasta 112
red capsicum, with seared tuna 199

Scallops with fresh fettuccine 175
Seared tuna with red capsicum sauce 199
Semolina, lemon, puddings with berry
    coulis 210-211
Soup
    baby pea and ham 163
    chunky vegetable, chicken and pasta
        168
    hearty winter vegetable 165
    pumpkin, sweet potato and cumin dhal
        167
    roast chicken, garlic and borlotti bean
        166
    sweet potato, carrot and ginger 164
Spaghetti with steamed greens 178
Spatchcock, lime and saffron on bulgur
    184
Spinach
    baby spinach salad 102
    in cooking 102
    with honey-soy dressing 102
Spiral noodles with smoked chicken and
    pine nuts 180
Split peas 115
Stir-fried greens 102
Stir-fry, vegetable and noodle 112
Stuffed eggplants 185
Summer pudding 213
Sweet potato
    carrot and ginger soup 164
    mashed 103
    potato and garlic mash 205
    roasted 103
    tasty wedges 103

Tart, carrot and thyme 189
Thai green chicken curry 193
Three bean and basil salad 169
Tofu chicken with snow peas and hokkien
    noodles 182
Tomatoes
    and olive vinaigrette 128

Roma tomato, mint and cucumber
    salad 170
salsa 104
sauce 104
slow roasted 104
Tuna
    lunchtime 121
    seared, with red capsicum sauce 199
    with vegie toss 121
Turkish hummus 161

Vegetables
    and noodle stir-fry 112
    chargrilled vegetables and beans with
        pasta 177
    chunky vegetable, chicken and pasta
        soup 168
    easy cooked greens 102
    hearty winter vegetable soup 165
    stir-fried greens 102
Vinaigrette, tomato and olive 128

Warm salad
    chickpea 116
    lamb 124
Wedges, tasty 103

ACKNOWLEDGMENTS

The authors would like to thank the following people and organisations
for permission to use the copyright materials included in this book:

Our American co-author, Tom Wolever, for material on
monounsaturated fatty acids and high protein diets
extensively quoted in Chapter 4. This material originally
appeared in *Nutrition Today*, April 1999.

NSW Department of Sport and Recreation, the Department
of Health and the National Heart Foundation for material on
walking for exercise used in Chapter 8.

Professor Dennis Calvert and colleagues for information
in the table on pp. 48–55

A Hodder book

Published in Australia and New Zealand in 2002
by Hodder Headline Australia Pty Limited
(A member of the Hodder Headline Group)
Level 22, 201 Kent Street, Sydney NSW 2000
Website: www.hha.com.au

Copyright © Jennie Brand-Miller and Kaye Foster-Powell
Recipes copyright © Lisa Lintner

First published by Hodder Headline Australia in 2000 as *The Glucose Revolution GI Plus*

NATIONAL LIBRARY OF AUSTRALIA CATALOGUING-IN-PUBLICATION DATA

Brand-Miller, Jennie.
The new glucose revolution : Lifeplan.
New ed.

Includes index.
ISBN 0 7336 16 00 3.

1. Glycemic index. 2. Dietetics. 3. Cookery
I. Foster-Powell, Kaye. II. Lintner, Lisa III. Title.

613.2

Designed and typeset by Seymour Design, Sydney
Photographs by Jennifer Soo
Printed by Australian Book Connection